GENDER-RELATED BEHAVIORS OF CHILDREN IN ABUSIVE SITUATIONS

by

Judith Martin, Ph.D.

Published by
R & E PUBLISHERS
P. O. Box 2008
Saratoga, California 95070

Library of Congress Card Catalog Number
81-86006

I.S.B.N.
0-88247-685-8

HV
741
.M346
1983   39,264

TABLE OF CONTENTS

TABLES

FIGURES

PREFACE

The existence of child abuse was discovered less than twenty years ago. Concern for the welfare of these children and their families has persisted and expanded since that time. It is hoped that this research, which examines some aspects of the child's role in abusive events, will contribute to our understanding of the dynamics of such behavior and suggest new methods for treating families undergoing these painful experiences.

The support and critical commentary provided by several individuals made this study possible. Dr. Alfred Kadushin expected careful consideration of alternatives and foretold completion of the project. Dr. Leonard Berkowitz offered suggestions and ideas that were invaluable to the end. Dr. Fredrick Seidl and Dr. Jack Westman discussed the needs of these families and the treatment they require. Dr. Joan Robertson assisted in organization and development of the information provided here. Finally, Jim McGloin helped with some of the nitty-gritty work, contributing to the project in ways that can never be repaid.

CHAPTER I

THE RESEARCH PROBLEM:
BACKGROUND AND THEORETICAL PERSPECTIVE

THE PROBLEM

This research is designed to contribute to knowledge about the role of the child in abusive situations by examining behaviors of boys and girls that precipitate abusive responses from their parents.

Exploration of the child's role in abuse is a topic of recent concern to researchers. In the past, the part played by parents in the development of this problem was over-emphasized. Children were viewed as "innocent victims" maltreated by adults with serious socio-emotional problems (Bakan, 1970; Boisvert, 1972; Delsordo, 1963; Laury, 1970). This approach is linked to a more general perspective on child development in which parents are considered the "bad guys," responsible for the destiny (and problems) of their children (LeMasters, 1970; Rosenthal, 1973).

In contrast, Kempe and Helfer (1972) suggest there are at least three factors that must be considered to obtain a complete picture of abuse: the abusive parent, the abused child and the environment in which abuse occurs. Little work has as yet been done to explore the role played by the last two of these factors. Impetus for study of the child's role is provided by Stella Chess (Bishop, 1971, p. 624), who states:

Given any degree of ambivalence (incomplete acceptance and therefore partial rejection) of the parent role, the characteristics of the child may foster and reinforce a specific direction of parental attitudes and practices.

In any situation where parents and children interact, Richard Bell (1968) argues, parents have a repertoire of possible behaviors they can use. The specific responses they utilize vary, depending on the type of stimulus the child brings to the situation. Research findings cited by Beckwith (1972), Yarrow and Waxler (1971) and others suggest the validity of this perspective. (See also Alexandrowizc, 1975; Parke, 1974; Robson & Moss, 1970; Schonell & Watts, 1956-7.) Impetus for the study of the role of the abused child is also provided by victimology research. Megargee (1969, p. 1076) finds that the behavior of perpetrators of crime combines with instigation from the target to produce violence. (See also Gelles, 1972; Schultz, 1968.)

The purpose of this research is to redress an imbalance in our knowledge of abuse by examining characteristics of the child, who "acts as a stronger stimulus for evoking that potential for physical abuse than other children might" (Martin & Beezley, 1974, pp. 73-74).

Research with this focus is necessary, not only because it provides a more complete picture of abuse, but also because it has utility for those in the helping professions who work with families in which such violence occurs. As Weinberger (1972, p. 150) points out, it is all too easy for the therapist to be biased in favor of the child. This does disservice to the child, for he "is not viewed as an active participant in his problems." Instead, clinicians view him as a helpless victim without power or responsibility for his own future. Knowledge of the part played by children in abusive situations encourages those in the helping professions to perceive abuse as a family problem and to consider the role of each family member in working to reduce the recurrence of abusive incidents.

ful, obedient and unrebellious, even when they are young babies. Abusive parents think that children should act like little adults. Their expectations are often impossible to meet, since the child frequently does not as yet have the cognitive or developmental capacities to respond appropriately to them. (See Baumrog, 1975; Galdston, 1968; Galdston, 1975; Gil, 1970; Helfer, 1973; Hurt, 1975; Paulson & Blake, 1969.) Steele and Pollock (1968) note that parents frequently make excessive demands on children in our society. However, child abusers are distinguished by the intensity and prematurity with which they apply their expectations in child rearing.

The intensity of these parental demands has been traced to ambivalence concerning their adequacy as parents, to use of the child's behavior as a measure of their own worth, and to their lack of knowledge about appropriate child rearing methods (Freeman, 1975; Galdston, 1975; Lord & Weisfeld, 1974). Unfortunately, the soft nature of this data, based as much of it is on assessment of a small number of clinical cases, makes such reasoning highly speculative. More rigorous research examining the etiology of these expectations and their role in abusive situations is needed.

Three other characteristics of abuse are of relevance for this study. Violent episodes frequently involve some behavior on the parts of the child that triggers an abusive response from parents. This behavior serves as a stimulus for parents already predisposed to act abusively (Parke and Collmer, 1975). Data substantiating this perspective was provided by Gil in his nationwide study of abuse. Paulson and Blake (1969, p. 90), citing Gil's research, state that initially, one of the most prevalent features of this type of event is that it involves severe disciplinary action by the attacker in response to perceived misconduct by the victim. In Gil's study (1970) 63% of the abuse incidents surveyed connected some immediate response to a specific act on the part of the child.

Another significant facet of abusive situations concerns the fact that, in many families, it is the behavior of one particular child to which parents respond with excessive discipline. Gil (1970) found that at least half of the children included in his survey had experienced previous abuse. However, siblings had been abused in only 27.1% of the cases. Leontine Young (1964) examining protective service records in seven locations throughout the United States, also concluded that one child in the family is often the only target for abuse.[1]

Clinicians have also uncovered evidence of repeated violence in families in which child abuse is identified. Although some of these incidents are one time occurrences, more typically, according to Gil (1971), they become part of a fairly stable pattern of family interaction. Gelles (1977, p. 17) in a study of a representative sample of American households, likewise states:

> While it is generally accepted that slaps, spankings, and shoves are frequently used techniques of child rearing, we find that even bites, kicks, punches and using objects to hit children occur frequently in the families where they are employed.

(See also Terr, 1970.)

Child abuse, as a developing pattern of interaction, is reinforced by the behavior of both the parent and the child. Parents justify their behavior by attempting to shift responsibility for the incident to the child. It is the child's naughtiness and stubbornness, they claim, that excuse their disciplinary excesses (Flynn, 1970; Galdston, 1975; Johnson & Morse, 1968; Laury, 1970; Parke and Collmer, 1975).

Abusive relationships are also perpetuated by the child who repeats behaviors that previously elicited abuse. Parental attempts to control behavior through the use of excessive discipline may produce the opposite result. The child may, instead, subsequently repeat that particular type of behavior.

Frankiel (1959), in a review of child development research, cites a finding of Sears, Maccoby and Levin: harsh punishment for a behavior tends to produce more, not less, of that behavior.

Hoffman (1970b), reviewing research on moral development of children, states that the use of power assertion as a disciplinary technique fails to teach the child to internalize moral rules. Children are, therefore, more likely to again break the same rules than they would be if other forms of discipline were used. Feshbach (1970) reports that severe parental punishment of aggression may inhibit or escalate that behavior. By frustrating the child and providing an aggressive model, parents may stimulate the child to act more aggressively. Straus (1971), reviewing studies conducted by Maccoby and Masters, describes a similar process occurring when parents punish children for dependent behavior.

To summarize, an abusive event is often perpetrated by a parent who holds excessive and premature expectations for his or her child. Frequently, the parent is responding to a particular behavior exhibited by one special child in the family. The incident is often part of an ongoing pattern of interaction between a parent and child, one in which behavior of the child repeatedly receives abusive responses from the parent. The parent perceives this behavior as one requiring discipline, thereby justifying his or her abusive acts; the child repeats the behavior because harsh punishment has not taught him or her to control it.

THE CHILD'S ROLE IN ABUSIVE SITUATIONS: EXISTING EVIDENCE

Data have been provided which suggest the child may play a role in abusive events by exhibiting or repeating some type of behavior that the parent is likely to respond to with excessive discipline. This evidence raises two basic questions concerning the child's role in such events. First, what specific behaviors of the child elicit abusive responses from the parent? Second, what role do basic characteristics of the child, such as gender, play in distinguishing between the types of behavior that trigger abuse? Information currently available to answer these questions is of two distinct types. It consists either of general reports of parents' justificatory statements made after the incident or of outside appraisals of the problematic characteristics of the child. These characteristics may or may not be exhibited during the abuse incident.

Bennie and Sclare (1969), in a study of ten abusive parents, found they complained that the children were too demanding, disobedient and deviant. Young (1964), in an analysis of protective service records, described similar parental concerns. The children "drove parents crazy," were "evil" or "freaks," and they refused to respond to discipline. Young discussed one specific behavior that served as a stimulus for abuse — soiling. However, she did not examine any other activities of children exhibited during the incidents. Green (1976), comparing abusive and neglecting parents, reported that abusive mothers were most likely to describe their children as self-destructive, aggressive, and as having school difficulties. However, Green did not discuss the role of these difficulties in abuse incidents.

Objective evaluations of these children suggest they exhibit a wide array of serious problems. Describing the past and present functioning of a nationwide sample of abused children, Gil (1970, p. 108) found a "level of deviance in excess of the level of any group of children selected at random from the population at large." Eight percent showed intellectual deviance; 14% had physical problems; 13% were in special education classes or operated below grade level; and three percent of the school-age children in the sample had *never* attended school. (See also Elmer, 1966).

Bishop (1971) reported that infants who are at high risk for abuse include the premature, congenitally malformed and twins. Elmer et al. (1971) found them deviant in growth, language, motor and social development. Abused babies cried excessively and had feeding problems. (See also Friedrich and Boriskin, 1961; Hurt, 1975; Martin, 1972.) Older abused children have been depicted as ugly, offensive and provocative. They are difficult to manage and tend to be either passive and withdrawn or angry (Elmer et al., 1971; Galdston, 1965; Galdston, 1975; Green, Gaines & Sandgrund, 1974; Hurt, 1975; Martin & Beezley, 1974; Terr, 1970). Johnson and Morse (1968, p. 149), in a study of 101 children described them as:

7

. . .hard to care for. They did not gratify the parents' self-image or were threatening to it because they failed to respond to care, to thrive, and to show normal growth and development. The child most likely to be damaged was the one who was overly active or who was the most difficult to supervise or care for.

Assessments by parents and by other more objective observers of abused children are in agreement. These children exhibit a range of serious problems making them difficult for adults to cope with. However, the role these problems play in specific abusive events has not been explored in these studies. Existing data do not, therefore, provide adequate information to answer the first question posed above; little is known about the behaviors of children that are likely to precipitate abuse.

Parke and Collmer (1975, pp. 36-43) do attempt to deal with this issue by suggesting several ways children *may* contribute to abusive interaction. Concerning infants, they list the following behaviors as potential stimuli for abuse:

1. Infant crying, when coupled with maternal inability to control it.

2. Lack of clarity and readability of infant cues.

3. Child's predispositions and preferred interaction styles, when these do not match mother's standards.

4. Lethargy, passivity.

5. Low birth weight infant.

For older children, the following characteristics are mentioned (pp. 43-45):

1. Lack of physical attractiveness.

2. Over- or under-activity.

3. Defiance.

Research is needed to discover the extent these actions *do* serve as precipitants in violent parent-child exchanges.

In examining the role of the child's gender in abuse it must first be noted that approximately equal numbers of boys and girls are abused. This finding is cited in studies from a variety of sources — a nationwide survey of reported cases (Gil, 1970), a ten-year review of reported cases in Wisconsin (Oghalai, 1977), a smaller study of hospitalized children (Lauer, TenBroeck & Grossman, 1974) and research on murdered children (Resnick, 1969). This fact is surprising in view of the developmental literature on gender differences in parental discipline, which reports that boys are disciplined (and more generally aggressed against) more often than girls. Parents are also more reluctant to punish girls than boys (Block, 1975; Gelles, 1977; Maccoby & Jacklin, 1974; Straus, 1971; Yarrow & Waxler, 1971).

The role played by the child's gender in violent incidents is not discussed in most abuse publications. With regard to parental views that deal with gender of the child we have found only two references. Gwendolyn Bell (1973) noted that parents complained their abused children were not the "right sex." Galdston (1975) in an evaluation of abusive parents participating in a special treatment program, found them overly concerned that lax discipline might lead to dire consequences. The parents feared their sons would otherwise become delinquent, their daughters promiscuous.

Two additional studies examined differences between abused boys and girls using more objective assessment techniques. Elmer et al. (1971) evaluated the mood, activity level, approach behaviors and distractability of maltreated infants. They found the male babies strikingly more negative in mood than their non-abused male peers. Abused girls, in contrast, were more positive in mood than their non-abused peers. The authors interpreted this finding as suggestive that male and female babies develop different

9

response patterns to abusive parental behavior. Galdston (1975), in his evaluation of the effectiveness of a day care project for abusive families, studied 34 male and 39 female children who ranged in age from six months to four years at the time they entered the program. The abused males were inclined to be violent, and this was one recognizable form of activity in the midst of otherwise bland and aimless behavior. Abused female children, on the other hand, were prone to autoerotic behavior. They sucked their thumbs, twirled their hair and rocked.

This literature suggests that differences exist in the behavior of abused boys and girls. However, data on the variety and extent of these differences is scant. Moreover, no research has been located which explores gender differences in the behaviors of children during the abusive event. The present study is designed to provide this missing information.

THEORETICAL PERSPECTIVE: THE CHILD'S GENDER AND BEHAVIOR IN ABUSIVE SITUATIONS

CONTEXT

As a context for the development of hypotheses concerning the contribution made by the child's gender in abusive interaction, this study will rely on theory and research findings from the child development literature. This literature has relevance for the present study, in part, because there is no clearcut line distinguishing abusive behavior from more normative forms of physical discipline frequently used by parents during the course of child rearing.

Normative discipline consists of various social control techniques used by nonabusive parents when punishing children. Unlike child abuse, these techniques are considered acceptable methods to be used in response to perceived misbehavior of the children. Martin Hoffman (1970b) classifies them into three types:

1.   Power Assertion: physical punishment, deprivation of

privileges or objects, use of force or threat of it.

2.   Love Withdrawal: parental expression of anger or disapproval.

3.   Induction: providing the child with reasons why behavior should be changed.

Physical discipline, one form of power assertion, is of particular importance, since it most closely resembles child abuse. It is a disciplinary technique pervasively used in American society. In a nationwide study of more than one thousand parenting relationships, Gelles found that 63% of his sample mentioned one or more episodes in which physical discipline had been used in the last year (1977). Korsch, Christian, Gozzi and Carlson (1965), in interviews with mothers bringing infants to a pediatrician, found that more than one-third punished children less than six months old, while one-half with babies six to twelve months old had spanked them. Straus (1971), in questionnaires given to students in their senior year of high school, found 24.6% said their parents often or always hit them or threatened to do so. Physical disciplining is such a common social control method that Gelles (1972, p. 58) labels it "normal violence," one of several "incidents of violence in the family that are routine, normative, and even thought of as necessary by family members."

Physical force is widely used because it produces rapid results; it places immediate restraints on the child's behavior. However, it is not a preferred disciplinary method. Its use does not teach children to generalize behavior rules to new situations; its effectiveness quickly wears off; and it can teach children to act aggressively, since parents provide aggressive models to imitate (Berkowitz, 1973; Gelles, 1972; Hoffman, 1970a; Lefkowitz, Walder & Eron, 1963). As Berkowitz points out (1962, p. 73):

The parent who relies primarily on his child's fear of punishment must be constantly on guard for violations of his rules. If the child sees that the

11

parent is not present and believes he can get away with some transgression he is all too likely to take the chance.

Abusive behavior can be placed on one end of a continuum that has, at its opposite end, very mild forms of corporal punishment (pats, for example). Society, through its social control agents, decides the point at which more moderate forms of such punishment (kicks, bites, shoves) become excessive, unacceptable, and, therefore, abusive. However, the line between acceptable and abusive discipline is not clearcut, and it is often difficult to distinguish between the two (Gil, 1970, Williams & Stith, 1974). Research on milder forms of violence towards children may, therefore, shed some light on the role of the child's behavior in eliciting abuse.

DISCIPLINE, PARENTAL EXPECTATIONS, AND GENDER OF THE CHILD

The 1971 White House Conference on Children (reported in Williams & Stith, 1974) defines the primary family task as the socialization of children. Socialization involves education in appropriate behaviors and attitudes for the gender, age and social status the child occupies relative to the culture in which (s)he lives (Clausen & Williams, 1963; Straus, 1971).

A primary component of socialization is social control. Through limit setting, physical punishment and other forms of normative discipline, children learn the rules for correct and incorrect behavior and gradually begin to apply these rules in controlling their own behavior (Feshbach, 1970; Hoffman, 1970b; Williams & Stith, 1974). In his description of physical discipline, Gelles (1972, p. 68) provides a picture of the process occurring here. An important feature, he says, is the:

> elaborate calculus that parents employ for deciding what type of behavior deserves what type of punishment. There are both implicit and explicit rules for

using violence that parents develop in interaction with their children that they expect their children to learn and to adhere to.

Parents, he adds, attempt to consistently enforce these rules in their day-to-day interaction with their children.

Parents also attempt to teach children rules for appropriate gender role behavior. Age and gender are the basic and most powerful role assignments in society, two of "the small number of core variables around which the structure of the personality develops" (Terman, 1976, p. 386). Social learning and modeling processes provide the primary means whereby children learn appropriate sex-linked behaviors and attitudes (Bandura & Walters, 1976; Maccoby & Jacklin, 1974). Parents are key figures in this process. It is their rewards and punishments that help shape the child's behavior in the appropriate direction. It is the characteristics they exhibit which provide the child with primary models for masculine and feminine behavior (Block, 1975; Kohlberg & Zigler, 1976; Maccoby & Jacklin, 1974).

Gender related expectations they hold for the child are also important. Parental expectations of the child in terms of appropriate behavior for that child's gender provide the standards against which the actual behavior of the child is judged acceptable or unacceptable.

These parental expectations are learned, in part, through punishment for behavior considered unacceptable, according to Murray Straus (1971). Straus argues that parents use punishment to train children in the roles they hope the children will occupy as adults. These roles differ for boys and girls. Boys, for example, are expected to need many more aggressive skills in their anticipated adult roles. Girls are, therefore, disciplined to behave less aggressively, boys to act with greater aggression. (See also Newman & Newman, 1975.)

Contrasting perceptions and expectations for male and female children are already apparent when children are very young. Goodenough (reported in Maccoby & Jacklin, 1974), conducting a study with parents of nursery school girls, found that one half of

13

the twenty parents interviewed described their daughters as sexy, soft, cuddly and flirtatious.

In an extensive examination of parental perceptions of children, Block (1975) carried out research with seventeen different samples, including 696 mothers, 548 fathers and 1227 young adults from the United States, England and Scandinavia. Using a questionnaire, she assessed gender-related factors in parental socialization behaviors. Despite wide variations in characteristics of the samples, Block found consistent differences in perceptions of male and female children and in reported behavior towards them. She concluded that her studies offer clearcut evidence of differential socialization of children, based on gender.

Gender-related expectations are linked to actual differences in the treatment of male and female children. Seavy, Katz and Zalk (1975) provided 42 subjects with an opportunity to interact with a three-month-old white female infant. In one of three experimental conditions, subjects were not told the baby's gender. At the close of the experiment, the authors found that discovery of the child's gender was highly important to these subjects. Moreover, the adults' assumptions as to the child's gender affected their behavior. Both their choice of a toy and the amount of physical contact they had with the baby varied, depending upon their assumption that it was a boy or girl. Based on these findings, the authors suggest that the actual behavior of the child may be less important than adult expectations in determining the interactions that occur. This observation has been questioned, however, by Barry, Bacon and Child (1976). In their study, they did not find parents treating male and female infants differently.

Research examining the connection between adult expectations and behavior of the child in disciplinary situations is rare. As we have previously noted, boys are disciplined by parents more often than girls. Maccoby and Jacklin (1974, pp. 330-331), in an in-depth review of gender-related developmental research, find that "with few exceptions boys receive more physical punishment than girls do." These results recur over a wide range of age groups. Parents also expect boys will have to be controlled more frequently than girls. (Block, 1975). No research has been located which examines the relationship between gender of the child and specific types of behavior for which children are punished. However, the existence of gender differences in behavior suggests that gender differences may exist in punished behaviors as well.

Both the similarities and differences between child abuse and other forms of discipline point to the relevance of gender-related issues in abusive situations. Abusive parents, like their normative counterparts, may discipline boys and girls for different types of behavior, based on their gender role expectations. Because abusive parents tend to have strong, rigidly structured expectations for children, this gender difference may be even more evident in abusive parent-child interaction than in other physical disciplinary situations.

SUMMARY

In this chapter, the importance of consideration of the child's role in abusive situations has been stressed. In an effort to understand some aspects of this role, this study will explore differences in the behaviors of boys and girls that precipitate abusive responses from parents.

Both the characteristics of normative disciplinary events and the special qualities of abuse suggest that the child's gender is a factor of relevance in determining behaviors likely to precipitate abuse. The contribution made by each of these factors is illustrated in Figure 1.

FIGURE 1

CHARACTERISTICS OF PARENTS AND CHILDREN THAT SUGGEST GENDER DIFFERENCES IN BEHAVIOR OF THE CHILDREN

CHILDREN'S
CHARACTERISTICS
Behavioral differences
between boys and girls

SUGGEST:
Gender differences in behaviors
requiring disciplinary response

SUGGEST:
Gender differences
in behavior precipi-
tating abuse

PARENTS'
CHARACTERISTICS
Gender-related expectations
translated into rules for
childrens' behavior

SUGGEST:
Differential parental response to
violation of expectations for boys
and girls

coupled with

Rigid, extreme implementation
of expectations by abusive
parents

FOOTNOTES

[1]The findings of two other studies are in conflict with these conclusions. Lauer et al. (1974) and Silver, Dublin and Lourie (1969) both report that a preponderance of cases they studied also showed sibling abuse. However, both of these studies examined only hospitalized abuse incidents and evaluated a much smaller sample of cases than Gil or Young did.

CHAPTER II

THE RESEARCH PROBLEM:
CONCEPTS AND HYPOTHESES

CONCEPTS

There are a variety of behavioral areas in which perceived and actual differences between boys and girls suggest gender differences in behaviors that may precipitate child abuse. These behaviors, the dependent variables of the study, are described below. In any study of gender differences, several other background characteristics of both the parents and children should be considered. In this research, the gender of the parent, age of the child and socioeconomic status of the family are secondary independent variables whose relevance for the study of gender differences is also discussed below.

GENDER-RELATED BEHAVIORS OF CHILDREN

The lack of available data on gender-related behaviors which precipitate punishment or abuse has led us to search the literature for all available information on gender differences in behavior of children. Two major information sources exist — that on parental expectations for their offspring and that examining the actual differences in behavior of boys and girls. When differential expectations are reinforced by actual differences in behavior, these gender related variations in terms of punishment also seem most likely to occur. These areas are summarized in Figure 2.[1]

Description of Behavior Categories

Aggression. Parents expect boys to be highly aggressive, to be rough, and to physically defend themselves. Boys, according to Kagan (1964), are given a "license" to be aggressive, while girls are specifically prohibited from doing so. (Berkowitz, 1973; Feshbach, 1970; Frodi, Macaulay & Thome, 1977; Maccoby & Jacklin, 1974).

One of the most well-documented conclusions in the developmental literature is that boys are more aggressive than girls, both verbally and physically. Gender differences in aggression begin early, possibly by age two, and are clearly evident by age five. They persist throughout childhood (Bandura & Walters, 1963; Block, 1976; Feshbach, 1970; Lefkowitz et al., 1963; Maccoby & Jacklin, 1974).

Active Behaviors. Like the term aggressive, active is an adjective parents frequently use to characterize boys. Boys are considered impulsive, noisy, interested in gross motor tasks. They are expected to involve themselves in rough and tumble play. Girls, in contrast, are expected to be quiet, reserved, "lady-like," and even passive in their behavior. They are discouraged from engaging in rough and tumble play (Bloc, 1975; Kagan, 1964; Maccoby & Jacklin, 1974). Again, expectations are in line with actual behavior. Already in infancy, males move more, are more irritable, and sleep less than females. Although activity levels vary greatly with age, boys are generally more active than their female peers throughout childhood. This gender difference extends to problematic areas as well; boys tend to be labeled "hyperactive" more frequently than girls (R. Bell, 1968; Block, 1976; Lapouse & Monk, 1968; Tyler, 1976. In disagreement, see Maccoby & Jacklin, 1974[2]).

Defiance. Defiance and conformity form two ends of a continuum. Defiance involves active failure to obey others; con-

FIGURE 2
BEHAVIOR CATEGORIES REFLECTING GENDER DIFFERENCES IN PARENTAL EXPECTATIONS AND CHILDREN'S BEHAVIOR

BEHAVIOR CATEGORY	PARENTAL EXPECTATIONS	CHILDREN'S BEHAVIOR
Aggression	Boys are to act aggressively, girls unaggressively	Boys more aggressive
Active Behaviors	Boys to be highly active, girls much less active	Boys more active
Defiance	Boys are to act defiantly, girls to be conforming	Boys more defiant, girls more conforming with adults
Expression of Emotional Upset	Girls to exhibit emotion, boys to hide it	Girls express more fear, anxiety
Achievement-Related Behaviors	Boys to be more achievement-oriented, successful, dominant than girls	Boys more dominant, competitive, find success more important, rewarding; girls do better academically
Social Behaviors	Girls to be more socially oriented, boys more object-oriented	Girls generally more sociable; no gender differences in more intimate relationships
Behaviors Reflecting on Personal Appearance	Girls to be more clean, neat, concerned with appearance than boys	Girls more concerned with appearance; no data on cleanliness
Performance of Household Tasks	Girls to be more helpful around the house than boys	Scant data makes conclusions risky
Sex-Related Behaviors	Girls to curb sexual activity, boys to indulge in it	Girls less sexually active in terms of intercourse; other differences unclear

formity is defined as active obedience to the rules and commands of others. Boys are described as "defiant when punished" and are seen as requiring extensive control for this reason. Girls, on the other hand, are seen as conforming, obedient and submissive (Block, 1976; Kagan, 1964; Maccoby & Jacklin, 1974).

Behavioral data reinforces this distinction. In research studies, girls are repeatedly found to be more responsive to discipline, more obedient to rules, more cooperative and compliant with adults. Boys are more disobedient in each of these areas. Maccoby and Jacklin (1974) point out that this gender-related distinction applies only to a child's relationships with adults. With peers, neither gender is clearly more conforming. (See also Barry et al., 1976; Becker, 1964; Block, 1976; Bronfenbrenner, 1961; Kohlberg, 1963.)

Expression of Emotional Upset. When they are frightened, worried or upset, girls are expected to show their feelings, boys to control and suppress them. Girls, therefore, are seen as more easily frightened and more willing to cry than boys (Block, 1975; Block, 1973; Kagan, 1964; Maccoby & Jacklin, 1974).

Jeanne Block (1976) reports that, in terms of actual behavior, female children do show more anxiety and fear than males. Maccoby and Jacklin (1974) find this especially true when self-reports are used to measure emotional upset. They suggest that boys believe they are not supposed to admit being afraid or worried, even though they do feel these emotions.

Behavior differences in the frequency with which the two genders cry are not so obvious. Studies of young children do not show persistent gender differences (Maccoby & Jacklin, 1974). Unfortunately, we were unable to locate any research on crying behavior of older children, although it is in the older age groups that one may more reasonably expect to find male-female variations if they exist.

Achievement-Related Behaviors. A variety of associated characteristics may be grouped under this heading, including activities suggesting the child is striving to be a success in life as

21

well as qualities perceived as necessary to attain this goal: competitiveness, dominance, leadership and achievement-orientation. In each of these areas, boys are expected to exhibit the behavior more readily than girls (Block, 1973; Block, 1975; Maccoby & Jacklin, 1974).

In actuality, boys exhibit more of some of these behaviors but not others. In terms of academic achievement, girls consistently perform better than boys. However, boys perform more adequately in competitive situations. Girls, in fact, may refuse to compete if their opponent is a male (Maccoby & Jacklin, 1974). Male children also find it more important to be a dominant member of their peer group. Maccoby and Jacklin report that there is a quality of "toughness" in the conception boys have of leadership, at least until they reach adolescence.

Children of both genders also find success a more acceptable situation for males than for females (Maccoby & Jacklin, 1974). Studies have found that both males and females evaluate successful girls more negatively than successful boys; male subjects are also less accepting of female success than girls.

In summary, significant achievement issues segregating male and female children in terms of expectations and behavior have to do with leadership, dominance, competitiveness and the general acceptability of success. It is acceptable for females to achieve. They are, however, discouraged from flaunting their ability by using it in competition with males or in attaining dominance over them. It is these particular aspects of achievement, not actual academic achievement itself, which produce gender differences in this category.

Social Behaviors. There are two levels on which girls are expected to perform better socially than boys. In general, in meeting and dealing with people, they are seen as more adept. Girls are expected to be friendly, poised, talkative and well-mannered. In more intensive and meaningful relationships, girls are also seen as faring better than their male counterparts. They are described as affectionate, affiliative, nurturing, sensitive to the feelings of others, warm and close (Block, 1973; Block, 1975; Kagan, 1964;

Maccoby & Jacklin, 1974). Boys are perceived as less interested and involved in social relationships and are expected to be less socially skilled. They are described as more object-oriented and interested in doing things rather than meeting people (R. Bell, 1968; Kagan, 1964; Maccoby & Jacklin, 1974).

On the more general level behavioral data paralled these findings. Girls are more polite, more concerned with saying the right thing, getting along well with others and being liked (Block, 1976; Maccoby & Jacklin, 1974). Girls also describe themselves as more sociable, while male children see themselves as more impersonal (Block, 1976; Newman & Newman, 1975; Tyler, 1976; in disagreement, Maccoby & Jacklin, 1974).

However, in more intense relationships, these differences are not so readily apparent. Close personal relationships are as meaningful to boys as to girls. Boys spend a great deal of childhood in interaction with peer group members, and they may, in fact, be more socially responsive to peers than female children are (Maccoby & Jacklin, 1974).

Personal Appearance. Girls are expected to be more clean and neat and more concerned with their appearance than boys. This difference is borne out in reality. According to Maccoby and Jacklin (1974, p. 343), "there is some evidence to support the view that girls continue to be much more interested in physical attractiveness than men and boys."

Performance of Household Tasks. Girls are generally expected to be more "helpful around the house" than boys (Maccoby & Jacklin, 1974). This expectation makes sense, since household tasks are generally considered to be women's work and girls may, therefore, require training in performance of such tasks. Only one study has been located which explores this issue. In cross-cultural research on sex roles of children in six societies, Whiting and Pope (reported in Block, 1975) found girls were more often assigned such domestic chores as looking after younger children, cooking and cleaning, food preparation and grinding.

Despite such scant information, we will include this area as one suggesting a source of possible gender differences in behavior of abused children, since household work is so frequently seen as a major responsibility of women.

Sex-Related Behaviors. It is interesting that data on parental expectations in the area of sexuality are very difficult to find. References to such behavior are frequently oblique. Jeanne Block (1975, p. 34), for example, notes that parents find it necessary to supervise daughters more carefully than sons. In explaining this she states:

> Restrictive parental behaviors are associated with, especially in the perceptions of daughters, parental anxiety, worry, and concern about the misfortunes that can befall young women as they grow up.

(See also LeMasters, 1970.)

Parents expect girls to inhibit sexual feelings and behavior, boys to express them. As Matteson (1975, p. 155) states, there is a double standard in terms of expected heterosexual behavior for males and females: "generally, the teen-age code restricts the girl to petting when the relationship involves affection, but this restriction is not expected to apply to boys." A girl, he says, is trained to be "genital-less and selfless," "treating her virginity as something to be preserved, as if she would be contaminated if she experienced her own sexuality" (p. 156; see also Kagan, 1964). Gender differences in overt sexual activity of boys and girls also have been documented, although these differences are diminishing.

David Gil, in his nationwide study of child abuse, found (1970) that more boys than girls are abused when under the age of twelve, but the situation is reversed for older children. Gil speculates that these teenage girls were frequently involved in altercations with their parents over their heterosexual relationships. Examination of this behavior category will allow us to test this hypothesis.

Gender Differences in Behavior

Comparison of parental expectations and children's behavior points to two basic types of relationships. For some categories parents expect children of one gender to engage in the behavior more frequently and the children do exhibit it more often than those of the opposite gender. These activities will be labeled *gender-consistent*. For boys, gender-consistent categories include: aggression, active, defiant and achievement-related behaviors; for girls, they include behaviors reflecting emotional upset, sociability, personal appearance and performance of household tasks. These actions are described in positive tones by parents. They are considered acceptable behavior, if displayed within broadly defined limits.

Gender-inconsistent behaviors include those acts which parents do not expect children of a given gender to engage in. The children also exhibit them less frequently than those of the opposite gender. Congruence between expectations and behavior is also found in these categories, although in a negative sense. They point out the "thou shalt nots" of gender role socialization (Block, 1973). Three areas are seen as gender-inconsistent for girls: aggression, active and defiant behaviors. One behavioral category is gender-inconsistent for boys. Although females are expected to exhibit fear and anxiety when upset, boys are expected to (and attempt to) control expression of such emotions.

Four behavioral areas are gender-consistent for children of one gender but are not gender-inconsistent for those of the opposite gender. Achievement issues are significant for boys. They are expected to be competitive, dominant and successful. Girls, however, are not specifically prohibited from achieving, even though they may not be encouraged to do so. Sociable behaviors and those involving personal appearance and performance of household tasks are gender-consistent for girls, but they do not reflect unacceptable behavior for boys. It is difficult to imagine boys being punished for doing the dishes or combing their hair, although parents may worry about the masculinity of sons who perform too readily in these areas.

Gender-consistent and -inconsistent behavior categories are

depicted in Figure 3:

FIGURE 3

GENDER-CONSISTENT AND GENDER-INCONSISTENT
BEHAVIOR CATEGORIES

BEHAVIOR CATEGORY	RELEVANCE FOR BOYS	RELEVANCE FOR GIRLS
Aggression	Consistent	Inconsistent
Active Behaviors	Consistent	Inconsistent
Defiance	Consistent	Inconsistent
Expression of Emotional Upset	Inconsistent	Consistent
Achievement-Related Behaviors	Consistent	
Social Behaviors		Consistent
Behaviors Reflecting on Personal Appearance		Consistent
Performance of Household Tasks		Consistent

Note: Sex-related behaviors are omitted from this table, since it fits into neither of the above categories.

Comparison of gender-consistent-inconsistent categories suggests possible differences in the actions of abused boys and girls in terms of both the type of behavior they display and the intensity of that behavior during abuse episodes. Since gender-consistent actions occur more frequently, parents are also more likely to be concerned with establishing what Bell calls "upper limit" and "lower limit" control of them (1968, p. 88). Use of upper limit controls involves a parental response designed to lessen or redirect the behavior of the child, since it exceeds "parental standards of intensity, frequency and competence for the child's age." Lower limit controls are utilized when the child's behavior falls below expected standards. Physical punishment, one type of control technique available to parents, can also be used in an attempt to regulate these gender-consistent behaviors.

The category of behavior may, therefore, differentiate between boys and girls in terms of the type of activity for which they subsequently experience abuse. Boys are likely to be abused for displaying aggressive, defiant, active or achievement-related behaviors, girls for issues involving emotional upset, sociability, personal appearance or performance of household tasks.

Within any one category, behavior may be consistent for children of one gender but inconsistent for those of the opposite gender. When this occurs, there may also be a difference between boys and girls in the intensity of the activity for which they are subsequently abused. Maccoby and Jacklin (1974) point this out with regard to aggression. Using Bell's terminology, the upper and lower limit controls for gender-consistent behavior are far apart, allowing for wide variations in behavior considered acceptable. Parents will punish expression of that behavior only when it is considered extreme enough to violate these relatively liberal rules. For gender-inconsistent behaviors, in contrast, parents are concerned with extinguishing the behavior or with keeping it within much narrower boundaries. Variations in behavior considered acceptable by parents exist within a much more restricted range. Much less intense expressions of such behavior should, therefore, elicit limit-setting controls, including physical punishment or abuse.

Frodi et al. (1977, pp. 43-44) reporting evidence for and against the proposition that "behavior which is given a neutral or a positive label of 'assertiveness' when seen in men may be seen as sick or excessive aggression in women," find "mixed support." The bulk of the studies they cite do suggest that intensity of behavior is a dimension distinguishing acceptable aggressive actions for males and females.

In this study, the possibility that intensity level differentiates between behavior of boys and girls in a variety of behavior categories will be explored. Boys are expected to exhibit more extreme forms of behavior precipitating abuse in situations where behavior is gender-consistent for them but gender-inconsistent for girls. These include the following categories: aggression, active behaviors and defiance. Girls are expected to be abused for more intense forms of emotional upset than boys.

In summary, behaviors precipitating abuse may be distinguished, based on gender of the child, in terms of the category of behavior (with gender-consistent behaviors being those most likely to elicit abuse) and within any one category of behavior, in terms of intensity (with gender-consistent behaviors being more intense than gender-inconsistent behaviors leading to abuse). Some reservations must be noted at this point. Because few clear facts exist in this area, we have used non-disciplinary developmental data and some speculative arguments in creating these predictions. They must, therefore, be considered exploratory hypotheses, preliminary guidelines for examining differences between boys and girls in perceived "misbehavior" during abusive situations.

A third type of relationship between parental expectations and children's behavior is suggested in Figure 2. It involves the category "sex-related behaviors." Interaction between parents and children with regard to this issue cannot be adequately understood using the analyses developed thus far. In this situation parents seem to be highly concerned with expression of the activity in girls, despite the fact that all available evidence points to greater sexual involvement among boys. As we have previously pointed out, parents seem to be very worried and anxious about expression of sexuality in their female children. This concern may lead them to discipline (and abuse) girls for this behavior more often than boys. The adequacy of this prediction will be tested in this study.

SECONDARY INDEPENDENT VARIABLES

Three additional factors are of basic importance in this study. They are the developmental level of the child, the gender of the parent and the socio-economic status of the family. The relevance of each of these variables for research on the influence of the gender of the child in abusive situations is outlined below.

Developmental Level of the Child

Some of the abuse literature assumes maltreated children are usually infants. However, extensive research on reported cases (Gil, 1970) finds a substantial proportion of the incidents involve children over the age of six. Three quarters of the children were three years of age or older in the Gil study. A ten-year summary of cases reported in Wisconsin between 1967 and 1976 (Oghalai, 1977) noted 69% were four years of age or older.

Gil (1970) points out that age and gender of abused children are related, as we have previously noted. While boys make up the bulk of the younger cases, girls are over-represented among adolescents. He speculates that gender role differences may explain this finding. Girls are abused less often as children because they are more conforming; however, their sexual maturity is accompanied by increased parental restrictiveness, which produces conflict and abuse. Incest may also play a role in abuse of adolescent girls.

Age is considered an important factor in any study of children. Along with gender, it is a basic reference point for ascription of roles and statuses. Parental perceptions of and behavior towards their offspring change as a function of the level of maturity of the children. Parental behavior in disciplinary situations also varies as a result of growth of the child (Parke & Collmer, 1975). This is due, in part, to the fact that children pose new problems as they pass through each developmental phase (Feshbach, 1970; Lapouse & Monk, 1968; Williams & Stith, 1974).

The developmental literature discusses three distinct phases of childhood. Early childhood begins with birth and continues until children begin school. During this period, children are highly dependent on parents and require extensive care and attention. At the same time, their intellectual and social immaturity place limitations on parents in terms of the types of discipline that can be effectively used. Simple commands and rules, consistently applied, are most productive; more complex disciplinary methods, such as provision of verbal rationales for avoiding misbehavior, are not fully understood by these children (Hoffman, 1970b; Hoffman, 1970a; Stone & Church).

Latency begins when children attend school. During this period, there is a sharp drop in children's dependence on parents and a corresponding increase in their dependence on peers. Stone and Church (1968) call these the "gang years." (See also Hartup, 1963; Maccoby & Masters, 1970.) Learning the rules and dealing with the dilemmas of social interaction are issues of special significance (Newman & Newman, 1975). Moral development also undergoes tremendous changes when children reach the age of four or five. They are now able to understand the difference between right and wrong and use this knowledge in assessing their own behavior. However, these children are still highly dependent on external control as a deterrent to misbehavior (Hoffman, 1970b; Kohlberg, 1964).

Disciplinary issues also differ for this age group when compared to younger children. Williams and Stith (1974, p. 92) suggest that this period is especially troublesome for parents:

> In the fourth, fifth and sixth grades, problem behavior reaches a peak: teasing, discourtesy, scuffling, rebelliousness, carelessness, untidiness, and disobedience.

Other common problems include: defiance, aggression against siblings, dawdling, temper tantrums, shirking responsibility, lying, sneakiness, breaking and spilling things, rudeness, lack of attention or cutting up in school, and vandalism.

Adolescence, the third developmental period, is a time of preparation for adulthood. Trying out — and failing in — adult roles provide significant learning experiences. Increasing independence from parents and the concomitant decline in adult control over their behavior are issues of salience (Bowerman & Kinch, 1959; Conger, 1973). True moral judgment first appears in adolescence. Children of this age are able to consistently use internal reference points in judging the correctness of their own behavior (Kohlberg, 1964).

Delineation of the changing characteristics of children at various developmental levels suggests some ways that age of the child affects discipline. Children at the various levels typically behave (and misbehave) in different ways. The effectiveness of social control techniques also changes depending upon the developmental stage of the child. Parents who rigidly enforce rules concerning outside activities when the child is young are likely to find their efforts frustrated if they continue to do so as the child matures. With increasing age, the child's growing need for independence and autonomy and his greater capacity to profit by the use of verbal reasoning make restrictiveness and physical discipline gradually more intolerable. (See Becker, 1964; Berkowitz, 1973; Walters & Stinnett, 1971.)

Gender role issues also vary, depending upon the age of the child. As children grow, these issues become increasingly salient. In a study of fifth and tenth grade girls, Barouch (1974) found the older females had significantly higher sex role socialization scores than their younger counterparts. In early childhood, gender role identity begins to develop. However, few behavioral differences between boys and girls are evident. Variations in aggressive behavior, one of the strongest gender differences, appear with consistency only after children reach the age of five (Maccoby & Jacklin, 1974).

Several authors argue that development of a gender identity is a primary task of latency (Gesell & Ilg, 1976; Kagan, 1964; Maccoby & Jacklin, 1974; Newman & Newman, 1975; Stone & Church, 1968). Gender-typed behavior begins, for boys, at about the age of four. For girls, behavior is more variable until the age of nine or ten. During early latency, children's perceptions of gender differences are stereotypic and rigid. Boys may refuse to engage in behavior they consider "girlish." The child's classification of behavior as gender-related is largely dependent on external evidence of gender differences, such as hair length and clothing styles. As children in this developmental group mature, their conception of gender roles becomes less stereotyped and more flexible (Lee &

Stewart, 1976).

In adolescence, children develop interest in peers of the opposite gender. During this time, gender identity becomes more stable; increasing divergence occurs in the behavior of males and females (Maccoby & Jacklin, 1974). Girls become more invested in social relationships, boys more concerned with success. Gender differences in aggressive behavior are more evident than they were in latency (Eron, Huesmann, Lefkowitz, & Walder, 1974; Rosenberg & Simmons, 1975).

Overall, then, the age of the child is an important consideration in understanding both parental disciplinary conduct and gender-related activities of children. This material discusses general behavior of boys and girls, but it would seem that it may be equally applicable to analysis of gender differences in behaviors of children during abusive events. Its utility will be tested in this research.

Gender of the Parent

The parent's gender, like the child's age, is a background factor frequently mentioned in studies of child abuse. Gil (1970) finds that mothers and fathers abuse children approximately equally often, if amount of time spent in the home is taken into account.[3] However, researchers disagree in their assessment of the relationship between gender of the abusive parent and that of the abused child. Using a sample of 96 hospitalized abused children, Paulson and Blake (1969) found mothers attacked girls more often than boys. In England, Skinner and Castle (1969) examined the social work records of 78 battered children and found no relationship between gender of the child and that of the parent.

The abuse literature implies that mothers and fathers abuse children for different reasons. When discussing causes of maternal abuse, authors suggest that personality problems are relevant; in evaluating paternal abuse, however, they note the role of financial and other work-related stresses (Bryant et al., 1963; Spinetta & Rigler, 1972).

In developmental writings, gender of the parent is also considered significant, in part because mothers and fathers appear to have differing degrees of investment in insuring that children fulfill gender role expectations. Fathers are more concerned about this issue than mothers. Reviewing a series of research studies that include male and female parents, Block (1973, p. 517) concludes:

> . . .the data from these studies suggest that the father appears to be a more crucial agent in directing and channeling the sex typing of the child, both male and female, than has been supposed.

(See also Zeldow & Greenberg, 1975.)

Fathers may also, therefore, more consistently abuse children for gender-related behaviors than mothers do.

Developmentalists have also noted cross-gender effects in the socialization of children. A number of studies have found that the parent of the same gender as the child is more authoritarian, more controlling and less benevolent than the cross-gender parent (Becker, 1964; Bronfenbrenner, 1961; Walters & Stinnett, 1971; Williams & Stith, 1974). This occurs, for example, when parents deal with aggressive behavior (Maccoby & Jacklin, 1974, pp. 325-326):

> . . .it is in the area of aggression more than any other sphere of behavior that we find evidence of cross-sex effects, with fathers being especially severe towards boys.

This finding may also apply to abusive situations, with mothers more likely to discipline girls for gender-related behaviors, while fathers do the same with sons.

Socio-Economic Status of the Family

Socio-economic status is the third background factor to be considered in this research. In his nationwide study, Gil (1970) found that abusive families are generally poorer than the rest of

33

the population. They contain an unduly high proportion of one-parent homes. Non-white and large families are over-represented in their ranks. Other research provides a similar picture of violent homes (Brocker, 1977; Skinner & Castle, 1969; Young, 1964).

The developmental literature also discussed family values and discipline as they relate to socioeconomic status. Clausen and Williams (1963) describe contrasting values held by lower and middle class families. The latter group stresses internal standards and looks at motives for behavior; the former places more emphasis on external standards and judges behavior by its consequences. These orientations make sense, the authors say, when one considers factors most likely to be important and problematic in the lifestyle of each class. Chilman (reported in Williams & Stith, 1974) adds that middle class families tend to emphasize the importance of education, social striving, thrift, delayed gratification and cleanliness more than lower class parents. The lower class, she says, is more impulsive and more fatalistic.

Lower class parents also tend to use power assertion as a disciplinary technique more frequently than other socio-economic groups, according to some researchers (Becker, 1964; Clausen & Williams, 1963; Walters & Stinnett, 1971). The middle class, they say, relies more heavily on supportive techniques and the use of reasoning. In his study of violence in the home, Gelles (1972) found both occupational status and income inversely related to the use of violence.

However, Erlanger questions these findings. Re-analyzing existing data, he concludes that socio-economic differences do exist, but they are weak and not uniform. They also tend to be confounded with racial effects. Erlanger also notes inconsistent results across the various social class groups. The most poorly educated whites show the highest rejection of spanking. Overall, he says (1974, p. 81):

> Given the data currently available, the best conclusion about the relationship between social class and the use of physical punishment is that there is indeed some correlation, but that it probably is not

strong enough to be of great theoretical or practical significance.

(See also Lefkowitz et al., 1963.)

Social class has also been shown to be related to gender role typing. The lower class is said to more rigidly socialize children, especially girls, to exhibit "correct" gender-related behavior (Kagan, 1964; Walters & Stinnett, 1971). In the poorer groups, then, one might also find greater differentiation between the behavior of boys and girls in abusive situations.

HYPOTHESES

Based on the theoretical perspective outlined above, the following hypotheses will be tested:

Hypothesis 1: Children of one gender are more likely to be abused for exhibiting behaviors consistent with gender role expectations than are children of the opposite gender. Boys, therefore, are more likely to be abused for aggressive, defiant, active or achievement-related behaviors. Girls are more likely to be abused for behavior reflecting expression of emotional upset, sociable behaviors, or those reflecting on personal appearance or performance of household tasks.

Hypothesis 2: In any one behavior category, children exhibiting gender-consistent behavior will be abused for more intensive forms of that behavior than will children for whom that behavior is gender-inconsistent. Boys, therefore, will be abused for more intense forms of aggressive, active or defiant behavior. Girls will be abused for more intense forms of emotional upset.

Hypothesis 3: Girls are more likely than boys to be abused when exhibiting behaviors involving sex-related issues.

Hypothesis 4: With increased age of the child, the gender differences outlined in the first three hypotheses will become more distinct. No significant gender differences will be found in early childhood; gender differences will appear in latency and increase in adolescence.

Hypothesis 5: When the father is the abusive parent, the gender differences outlined in the first three hypotheses will be more evident than when the mother is the abusive parent.

Hypothesis 6: When the abusive parent is of the same gender as the child, gender differences outlined in the first three hypotheses will be more distinct than when the abusive parent is of the opposite gender.

Hypothesis 7: The lower the social class, the more evident are the gender differences outlined in the first three hypotheses.

FOOTNOTES

[1] Data on parental expectations come from few sources, cited in the text. Information on behavior differences between boys and girls is gleaned from a much larger number of sources. We have relied heavily on the summary of the literature produced by Maccoby and Jacklin (1974) and the re-analysis of that same data by Jeanne Block (1976). The literature on parental expectations suggests two other areas where parents expect different things from boys and girls. However, these differences are not reflected in the behavior of male and female children. These areas, having to do with moral development (boys lie more than girls) and dependency (boys are more independent, girls more dependent) are not, therefore, included as categories for study.

[2] In this and other behavior categories discussed below, there are several instances in which Maccoby and Jacklin (1974)

come to conclusions contradictory to those cited in this paper. When this occurs, references to their text will be preceded by the notation, "in disagreement." Block (1976) has raised such serious questions concerning the adequacy of their work that, in those instances where Block concludes that gender differences exist but Maccoby and Jacklin disagree, greater reliance is placed on the findings of Block.

[3]Developmental data might also support this finding. Although fathers are perceived as more powerful and more punishment-oriented, mothers are seen as having much more responsibility for raising children. Both, therefore, may be equally likely to punish children, although for different reasons. See Becker, 1964; Herbst, 1952; LeMasters, 1970; Strodtbeck, 1958; Walters & Stinnett, 1971.

CHAPTER III

METHODOLOGY OF THE STUDY

RESEARCH DESIGN

The research design used in this study is described by Campbell and Stanley (1973) as the "static group comparison." Using data on reported cases of child abuse in Wisconsin, gender of the child (the independent variable) is compared with the type of behavior that the child engages in during the abusive event (the dependent variable).

What this design lacks in terms of control over variables is compensated for in breadth of coverage. The design does not allow for examination of causal relationships, since the independent variable cannot be manipulated. Using this design, then, factors leading parents to differentially abuse boys and girls must be presumed to exist. Their presence cannot be assessed in this study. However, the design does allow for choice of a large representative sample of subjects. One can, therefore, generalize results to some larger population with a fair degree of confidence.

This pre-experimental type of design is appropriate for use in the present study. Conditions precipitating abuse are difficult to reenact in a laboratory setting, where greater control over causal factors is possible. Abusive events are more appropriately examined as they occur naturally.

that abuse. Invisibility of the child's injury and difficulties in reaching the family are but two of the many factors that help produce this type of situation (Broeckner, 1977).

These events are likely to produce a sample in which the poorer, more disorganized families in the community are over-represented. Reporters find it easier to refer such families, and social workers are apt to have prior contact with them and to investigate them more readily. Wealthier parents are likely to be under-represented, as are those who, in the eyes of the youth community, appear to be the solid, upstanding citizens. The sample is also likely to be biased by over-representing cases in which severe injury occurs to the child.

> Staff No. 1: Jan, let go of your feelings and accept the love in this room.
>
> Staff No. 2: I can't cause I'm scared. I'm scared to feel ... and I'm not worth it.

DATA COLLECTION PROCEDURES

Data for the study were collected from existing records. Reporting forms used by the state of Wisconsin for suspected abuse cases include a variety of items to be completed by the investigating social worker. Some of these items deal with background information on the parents and child. Others ask for a description of the incident, its causes and consequences. A copy of this form is included in Appendix A.

until the youth is pushed to respond for herself. She is told to reject whatever response that Staff No. 2 makes for her if it seems incorrect. Frequently, the youth identifies the staff's voice as her own and is pushed into a cathartic response ... appropriate follow-up discussion. Such encounters generally end with verbal and ... messages of caring ...

MEASUREMENT OF VARIABLES

DEPENDENT VARIABLES: BEHAVIOR CATEGORIES

Nine behavior categories have been designated for the study of gender-related actions of abused children. Measures for each category are based on the social worker's response to Question 41 on the state form. The question reads:

Please add a paragraph on ...
1) What precipitated the alleged abuse.
2) The alleged abuse incident.

Operational definitions take into consideration the limited amount of information available and are designed to make maximum use of those data.

Aggression

Berkowitz (1973, p. 97) describes aggression as an act with an intent and a goal. He sees it as a "behavior the goal-response to which is the injury of the person to whom it is directed." Other researchers (Bandura & Walters, 1963; Feshback, 1970) offer substantially the same definition.

Measures of aggression usually include verbal and physical categories (Maccoby & Jacklin, 1974; Yarrow et al., 1968). In this study, aggressive behavior will be further differentiated according to the target against whom it is directed — adults or other children. Assuming that physical aggression is more extreme than verbal and that aggression directed at adults is more serious, in the eyes of parents, than is such behavior directed at other children, a classification of this behavior in three categories of decreasing intensity is suggested:

1. High intensity aggression: physical aggression directed at adults.

2. Moderate intensity aggression: verbal aggression directed at adults; physical aggression directed at peers.

3. Low intensity aggression: verbal aggression directed at peers.

Active Behaviors

Maccoby and Jacklin (1974) outline a variety of ways to depict activity level of the child. For the purposes of this study, this term will be used to describe any movement of the child's body such that the child is perceived as moving "too much" or

41

"too little."

In devising an operational definition for this concept, we are again concerned with measuring both the behavior and its intensity. Intensity measures used for aggressive behavior are not applicable in this situation.

The following alternative measures will be used:

1. High intensity activity: child is described as persistently active; considered hyperactive, on the go all the time.

2. Moderate intensity activity: child displays milder forms of body movement upsetting to parents, such as fidgeting, drumming fingers on table.

3. Low intensity activity: child moves too slowly, is lethargic; takes hours to get up in the morning, lies around all the time.

Defiance

Defiance includes any overt refusal to obey commands or rules set down by parents or other adults (Maccoby & Jacklin, 1974). Operationally, this concept is measured by reference to key terms, such as, "refuses to" or "won't" used to describe the child's behavior. For behavior to be considered defiant, information on the abuse reporting form must suggest that the child is actively choosing to disobey the parent.

Intensity of defiance is measured by reference to the persistence of the child's behavior in the face of repeated efforts by the adult to make the child alter it:

1. High intensity defiance: any refusal of the child to obey, when accompanied by notation that the adult has tried two or more times to force the child to do so.

2.   Moderate intensity defiance: any refusal of the child to obey, accompanied by notation that the adult has given only one command to the child to do so.

Expresssion of Emotional Upset

This category includes any overt expression of distress, fear or worry on the part of the child. Operationally, persistence is, again, used to measure intensity:

1.   High intensity emotional upset: any crying, fear, worrying, anxiety or other forms of emotional upset accompanied by description of the behavior as persisting over time.

2.   Moderate intensity emotional upset: any description of such behavior with no indication of persistence over time.

Achievement-Related Behaviors

This category includes any behavior of the child that is inappropriate in competitive or leadership situations or that indicates failure to exhibit the appropriate amount of dominance or success in academic or other situations. Operationally, the following types of behavior are included:

1.   Failure to succeed: cannot learn properly, does not get boy scout merit badge, etc.

2.   Failure to exhibit appropriate competitive spirit: refuses to or cannot win or gracefully lose in situations where the child is struggling against others in an effort to win.

3.   Dominance or leadership problems: not exhibiting sufficient dominant behavior or excessive dominance;

a sissy or a bully.

Sociable Behaviors

This category includes actions considered ill-mannered, inconsiderate, rude or otherwise inappropriate in a social setting. The word "uncouth" depicts the flavor of these behaviors, which are apt to embarrass parents when displayed in front of others. This category also includes indicators of the child's general inability to get along well with others, despite parental expectations that he or she should be able to do so.

Examples of behaviors included in this category are:

1. Failure in social manners: child is impolite, rude, talks out of turn, picks nose in public.

2. General failure in social abilities: child never seems to have any friends, always fights with siblings, is too withdrawn.

Personal Appearance

Personal appearance items concern the presentability of the child in terms of bodily condition or dress. Operationally, behaviors comprising this category include dirty or unkempt clothing, hair or skin and clothing considered inappropriate by the parents. Descriptions of the child as "unattractive" are also included.

Performance of Household Tasks

Failure to complete routinely assigned or generally expected household chores are the focus of attention here. Operationally, the child's failure to adequately carry out babysitting, housecleaning or dishwashing chores are examples of such difficulties.

Sex-Related Behaviors

Activities described as "sexual" on the abuse reporting form and other behavior problems, arising out of the child's involvement in dating or marriage, are considered in this category. Operationally, the following are included:

1. Sex play, self-examination, masturbation.

2. Dating issues relating to length of date, person child is dating, places child goes on date, age when dating occurs.

3. Problems arising out of child's engagement or marriage plans.

4. Issues surrounding intercourse, pregnancy, venereal disease.

5. Sexiness or seductiveness of child, considered problematic for the parents or other adults.

SECONDARY INDEPENDENT VARIABLES:
Developmental Level of the Child

The three developmental stages of interest; early childhood, latency and adolescence, have already been fully defined. Although developmental level is more adequately measured through assessment of a variety of characteristics of the child, limitations in available data in the present study force us to use age of the child as a rough indicator.

There is some disagreement among researchers as to the exact ages to include in each of the three categories. Some consider thirteen-year-old children adolescents, while others describe them as still in latency (Group for the Advancement of Psychiatry, 1966; Williams & Stith, 1974). We will use the distinctions chosen by Stone and Church (1968). Children younger than six are in early childhood; those thirteen or older are adolescents.

Age was measured by reference to item seven, "Child's Birth Date" on the abuse report form, by comparing it with the date on which the reporting form was filed with the state.

Gender of the Parent

Gender of the abusive parent was determined by reference to item fourteen on the abuse report form. This item asks for the age and sex of the abuser.

Socio-Economic Status of the Family

Socio-economic status, according to Deutsch (1973), is an indicator of the family's economic and social milieu. SES is a measure that suggests the adult's lifestyle and value system, thereby indicating some of the major environmental and experiential stimuli affecting children in the home.

SES is typically measured through consideration of both the occupation and education of the child's parents (Deutsch, 1973). In this study, we followed this convention. The social class of the family was determined using a "Two-Factor Index of Social Position" developed by Michael Lamb (no date). Lamb's Index gives weighted scores to the occupation and educational level of the head of the household and then places the family into a social class by combining these scores. Although other, more sophisticated methods for measuring social stratification are available (see, for example, Hauser & Featherman, 1977), the data available in this research would not provide sufficient information to apply such methods. The Lamb Social Class Index has been validated using factor analytic procedures.

Weights from one to seven were assigned to various occupations by Lamb. Slight differences between report form categories and those used by Lamb led to use of the following weighted measures in this research:

1.   Higher executives, proprietors of large concerns,

major professionals.

2.5   Business managers, administrative personnel, proprietors of medium and small businesses, lesser and minor professionals.

4.   Clerical and sales workers, technicians, owners of little businesses.

5.   Skilled manual employees.

6.   Machine operators and semi-skilled employees.

7.   Unskilled employees, homemakers, unemployed.

Lamb also developed a seven-point educational scale, assigning weights based on the number of years and type of school the person had attended. Educational categories on the Wisconsin abuse report form are, again, slightly different, necessitating reassignment of weights as follows:

1.5   College graduate.

3.   Some college.

4.   High school graduate; vocational school in lieu of high school.

5.5   9-11 years of schooling.

7.   8 years or less of schooling.

These changes in Lamb's weighting system mainly affect those in the higher status occupational and educational groups. This does not create serious difficulties, however, since as we will point out elsewhere, few families in the study come from these higher status groups.

Social class is determined by using the following formula:

(Occupational weight x 7) plus (Educational weight x 4)

Resulting scores range from 11 to 77. They are grouped to form social class positions in the following manner (Lamb, no date):

Social Class	Range of Computed Scores
I	11-17
II	18-27
III	28-43
IV	44-60
V	61-77

The index, labeled Family Social Class in the study, provides the primary measure of socio-economic status in the research. Data on occupation and education were obtained by reference to items 19 and 20 on the abuse report form; "Father or Substitute's Occupation/Education" and "Mother's or Substitute's Occupation/Education". Data on the father were used whenever they were provided; when missing, the mother's information was used under the assumption that the father was likely to be absent from the home in such cases.

A second measure of socio-economic status involved assessment of the occupation of the abuser (item 28 on the report form). Unlike the Family Social Class measure, which provides information on the general social status of the family, this indicator evaluates the status of the particular parent who reacted abusively to the child.

INDEPENDENT VARIABLE: GENDER OF THE CHILD

Gender of the child was measured by reference to question eight on the abuse reporting form. This question asks the reporter to list the child's sex.

BACKGROUND DATA

The state reporting form contains other information on each case which is useful in more fully describing the characteristics of the sample under study. Included is information on the parent and child (race, previous abuse), aspects of the abusive event (methods used to abuse the child, resulting injury and medical attention), and agency involvement with the case (services provided, court proceedings). This material will also be used to evaluate representativeness of the sample.

SCORING PROCEDURES

To determine the correct labeling of dependent variables in the study, each abuse case was examined once to determine whether the child displayed aggressive behavior, reexamined with reference to activity level, and so on down the list of behaviors. In one abuse incident, several of these categories may be indicated. No attempt was made to choose one category as representative of all the child's activity during that incident. For example, the following statement:

> Child refused to stop fighting with his brother. He
> has not been getting along well with his brother for
> some time.

was classified as involving three different types of behavior: moderate aggression (fighting with brother), moderate defiance (refused to stop) and sociable behavior (has not been getting along well for some time). This scoring procedure raises problems in terms of orthogonality. Because different aspects of the same behavior may be assigned to more than one category, scores across the various categories are not additive.

RELIABILITY AND VALIDITY

Validation involves assessment of the adequacy of indicators chosen as measures of a concept. In common with other research using existing records as data sources, this study has three basic problems in terms of validity. (See, for example, Sellin, 1962.) First, data on the child's behavior during the abuse incident is incomplete. Available information consists of one or two sentences describing the event. It is highly unlikely that this brief account contains a full description of the child's role in the situation. As a consequence, results of the study reflect only the information the reporters have chosen to include on the form.

Second, the reports do not indicate the sources used to collect data. The description of the incident could have been obtained from the parents or the child. It may also result from "hunches," assumptions made by the protective service worker. Sources across the various cases in the sample are probably not consistent. This creates measurement problems because conflicting descriptions of the actions of the child could probably be obtained from each of the participants in and observers of the situation.

Finally, data for the study is compiled by a number of different protective service workers. It is questionable whether they attribute common meanings to the terms used to describe incidents under investigation. Observing the same act, one worker may label it hyperactive while another perceives it as fidgeting.

All of these factors raise questions that must be addressed in order to assume that true measures of concepts are obtained. Validation usually involves some evaluation of other available data on subjects, data believed to be correlated with the variables of the study. One determines whether this "external" information is associated with known material on sample subjects (Kerlinger, 1973). In this research, available material comes only from the abuse reporting forms. On these forms, only one other item deals with the child's behavior during the incident. Question 33 lists several possible "Stresses Just Before the Incident." Among them are four items relating to the child's contribution:

> Incessant crying
> Disobedience
> Hostility or Provocation
> Other child behavior (specify)

These options are too few to allow for comparison with the measuring schema used in this study. To rectify validity problems, a follow-up study should be conducted. Abusive parents should be interviewed and a full description of the child's behavior during the abuse episode obtained. This research is considered a preliminary study, designed to explore hypotheses which can subsequently be tested in research using more carefully controlled procedures.

Reliability, the accuracy or precision of a measure, can be evaluated in this study. Data on the dependent variables were assessed using two independent coders (the author and a Ph.D. student in Social Work). Coding procedures were refined after practice using a small number of cases and consultation in those areas where disagreements arose.

Inter-rater and intra-rater reliability tests were conducted, using the percent of cases in which agreement was obtained. Using the two-sample Z test (Marascuilo, 1971), agreement was better than chance in all cases. Inter-rater reliability was 95% or better for all dependent variables except aggression (91%) and defiance (89%). Intra-rater reliability was even higher, with defiance again showing the least amount of agreement (89%).

Reliability of measures of independent variables was also examined. Since the student who originally coded this data was unavailable to reassess cases, only inter-rater reliability is noted. Again, all Z-tests are significant at the .05 level, and the proportion of cases in which agreement was obtained was 90% or higher for each of the variables. Inter-rater reliability of measures of background variables was also satisfactory. Agreement was found in more than 90% of all cases for every variable except occupation of the person reporting the abuse (83%).

Although validity of measures is questionable in this study, due to the limited amount of information available and problems arising from use of existing records, reliability of measures used to assess independent and dependent variables is adequate in all cases.

DATA ANALYSIS

STATISTICAL PROCEDURES

The nature of the measurement indices places severe restrictions on the range of statistical tests that may be used. This research looks at the relationship between a nominal independent variable and dependent variables that are either nominal or ordinal scales with two- or three-point ranges. In consideration of these limitations, chi-square tests of homogeneity seem most appropriate. The chi-square test was developed for use with nominal measures and is ideal for use with scales that have a small range of values. One-tail tests are used, since each of the hypotheses is directional.

Limitations

Chi-square tests may not be used when expected values in table cells fall below ten (two-by-two tables) or five in larger tables (Siegel, 1956). In cases where this occurs, the Fisher Exact Test is an appropriate substitute.

Chi-square tests also prove problematic when inter-relationships among three or more variables are assessed and one is attempting to interpret direction of effects. Use of chi-square under these circumstances requires generation of a large number of tables (one for each category of the control variable), and determination of statistical significance is highly sensitive to variations in sample size from category to category. To aid in interpretation of results under these conditions, partial correlations have also been computed. The nominal nature of the data violates a basic assumption for use of this test statistic, but results (Chapter V) indicate congruence between findings using this procedure and the chi-square test in almost every instance. Chi-square remains the primary test statistic used in the study.

Significance Level

The alpha level for the entire study is .40. With experimentwise alpha set at this level, the rejection region for individual hypotheses is as follows. For hypotheses one and three, alpha is .10 overall. Nine comparisons are made under these hypotheses, thereby setting alpha at .011 per comparison. This provides a fairly conservative test of the basic hypotheses of the study. Given the large sample size used, this also helps to insure that statistically significant findings will have some practical significance as well.

For hypothesis two, alpha is .10 overall. Four comparisons are made under this hypothesis, setting alpha at .025 per comparison. For hypotheses four through seven, alpha is .20 overall. Twenty comparisons are made under these hypotheses, setting alpha at .01 per comparison.

Findings whose probabilities are at or below these alpha levels will be considered significant. Findings whose probabilities are slightly higher than these levels will be labeled suggestive.

CHAPTER IV

CHARACTERISTICS OF THE SAMPLE*

Applicability of results of the study to abusive situations in general is dependent upon the representativeness of the particular sample used in the research. This is one topic considered in this chapter. Description of some major characteristics of the sample is the second topic. Background data on the parents, the children, the abusive event and agency response to the situation will be considered. Available information also provides an opportunity to evaluate the degree to which some of the primary aspects of abuse outlined in Chapter I are found in this particular group of cases.

DESCRIPTION OF THE SAMPLE

FAMILY CHARACTERISTICS

830 abused children were included in this study. Slightly less than half of them (44%) were boys. Approximately one-third (29%) were below the age of six, while 35% were in each of the two remaining age groups — latency (age 6-12) and adolescence

---

*Note: These 830 children and their parents were also described in A. Kadushin & J. Martin. *Child Abuse: An Interactional Event.* NY: Columbia Univ. Press, 1981.

(age 13-17). The mean age of these children was 9.1 years.

Boys were younger than the girls in the sample. While more than half (58%) of the infants were male, three-quarters of the adolescents were females (Table 1).

TABLE 1
GENDER AND AGE OF THE ABUSED CHILDREN

| | | AGE | |
GENDER	INFANCY	LATENCY	ADOLESCENCE
MALE	57.9%	54.1%	25.1%
	(135)	(153)	(71)
FEMALE	42.1%	45.9%	74.9%
	(98)	(130)	(212)
TOTAL:	100%	100%	100%
	(233)	(283)	(283)

Chi-Square = 70.51, d.f. = 2; p = .0000
31 Cases Missing

Four out of five of the children were white and 14% were black. Small numbers of Native American, Latin American and Asian American children were also abused. Non-whites were over-represented among latency-age children. Although 20% of all the children were non-white, 29% of those aged 6-12 were non-white. White children, on the other hand, were more likely to be adolescents. 88% of all teenagers were from this racial group.

Abusive parents in the sample were slightly more likely to be fathers (59%) than mothers (41%). Most of them (83%) were natural parents of the child. 15% were stepparents, and 2% adoptive parents. There were significant differences between racial groups in the gender of the parent most likely to abuse the child. While two-thirds of white abusers were fathers, two-thirds of non-white abusers were mothers. These parents were not especially young. Only 15% were younger than 25, while 22% were 40 or older (Appendix B, Table 1). The mean age of these parents was 32.

There was no difference between mothers and fathers in the gender of the child they abused. However, male and female parents did tend to abuse children from different age groups. Until adolescence, mothers and fathers were equally likely to be violent, but father was three times as likely to maltreat the teenage child (Table 2). Fathers abused 70% of the teenage girls and 75% of the teenage boys in the sample.

TABLE 2
GENDER OF THE PARENT AND AGE OF THE CHILD

GENDER OF PARENT	AGE OF CHILD		
	INFANCY	LATENCY	ADOLESCENCE
MALE	50.6%	53.2%	71.0%
	(118)	(151)	201)
FEMALE	49.4%	46.8%	29.0%
	(115)	(133)	(82)
TOTAL:	100%	100%	100%
	(233)	(284)	(283)

Chi-Square = 27.56, d.f. = 2; p = .0000
30 Cases Missing

Families in the sample were, for the most part, poor. Of the 633 cases for which sufficient data were available to compute family social class, only 10% were from upper or middle class groups (Classes I-III). 61% were from the lowest social class group. Black, Native American and Latin American families were among the poorest in the sample. More than one-quarter of the Native American and Black fathers were unemployed at the time the abuse occurred. More than half of these fathers and three-fourths of the Latin American fathers had not completed high school.

Abusive mothers and fathers represented quite different types of occupations. Male abusers came from all occupational groups, although their most typical form of employment was unskilled labor (32%). Fifteen percent of these fathers were unemployed. None of the female abusers were executives or major professionals. In contrast to the men, they were most likely to be homemakers (56%) or clerical workers (10%). 13% of the women were unemployed. Despite the generally low occupational status of most of the abusive parents, abusive mothers had jobs with significantly lower status than the fathers. 11% of the males were professionals or owners of businesses, while only 3% of the female abusers are so employed (Appendix B, Table 2). There was no difference between abused boys and girls in the economic situation of their families.

Low income and few job skills are handicaps faced by many of these families. The protective service worker noted financial problems as a signficant stress factor for 45% of them. Additional economic burdens posed by a large family were also evident. More than one-third of the homes (38%) had six or more family members. Other non-economic stresses noted by the worker include health or mental health problems (29% of the cases) and general adjustment problems on a personal or community level (87% of the cases).

In summary, the "typical" abused child in the sample was a white girl or boy, nine years old, although abused children came from all age and racial groups. Younger children were more likely to be male, while adolescents were usually girls. The "typical" abusive parent was the natural father of the child, white, and in his early thirties. Again, however, these parents came from all age and racial groups and were almost as likely to be mothers as fathers.

Description of the parents and children in the sample suggests a wide range of characteristics they display. This does not hold true when one examines the economic status of these families. The overwhelming majority of them were poor. Fewer than one in ten came from the higher social class, occupational or educational groups. The families struggled with a variety of financial stresses and many faced problems on a personal or community level as well.

THE ABUSE INCIDENT

Most abuse incidents in this sample involved beating the child, either with the hand (36%) or with an instrument (45%). Fathers were more likely to use their hands, mothers to use instruments (Appendix B, Table 3). Other methods of inflicting injury on the child were used infrequently. Children were pushed, dropped or thrown in 69 cases (9%), strangled, suffocated or burned in 28 instances (4%) and kicked in 31 cases (4%). Incidents involving biting, tying up, shooting or stabbing the child were extremely rare. As a group, they comprised only 3% of the events. Psychological abuse did not frequently accompany physical maltreatment. It occurred in only 18% of the incidents.

Injury to the child was usually minor. Four-fifths had bruises or welts. 71 (9%) had abrasions, while 44 (6%) were cut. The more severe types of injury (fractures, suffocation, burns) were inflicted on less than five percent of the sample. Five of the 830 children died as a result of their injuries. Despite the fact that mothers and fathers differed in the methods used to inflict injury, there were no significant differences between them in the type or seriousness of injuries sustained by the child. The minor nature of the harm done to most of these children explains why 86% of them received no medical care following the episode. 47 children (6%) were hospitalized.

Parents did not use different methods to abuse boys and girls. However, the age of the child was clearly correlated with both the abuse method used and the extent of harm resulting from it. Children younger than six were most likely to be beaten with the hand (43%) while older children were more likely to be beaten with an instrument. Tying up or throwing the child was most likely to be used when he or she was young, while those older than five were more likely to be kicked (Appendix B, Table 4). Younger children were also more likely to sustain severe injury.

Fractures, burns or suffocation was suffered by 10% of the infants, 5% of those of latency age, and only 1% of the teenagers (Appendix B, Table 5). Half of the children younger than six required medical attention, in contrast to one-third of the adolescents.

Examination of these incidents suggests that parents usually used abuse methods most closely akin to more generally accepted forms of physical punishment — beating the child with the hand or an instrument. The more extreme (and unacceptable) the method, the less likely it was to be used. Few of the cases consisted of horrible, brutal forms of child battering often depicted in the media. Most of the children received bruises or welts and did not need medical attention for their injuries.

The literature also tends to emphasize abuse of the very young. Although they do not comprise the majority of children in this study, the serious nature of the injuries they sustain does justify strong community and professional concern about their welfare.

The abuse reports described four sources of stress that serve as precipitating factors in abuse. In 12% of the cases, parents were reacting to pressures evolving from family break-up or job difficulties. In 25%, an argument or physical fight precipitated the abuse. Parents were under the influence of alcohol or other drugs during 14% of the episodes. There were no significant differences between mothers and fathers in their experiences with these various difficulties except in the instance of drug use. Fathers were almost twice as likely as mothers to be under the influence of alcohol or other drugs at the time the incident occurred. For 10% of the female abusers and 17% of the males, drug use was evident (Chi-square = 7.75, d.f. = 1, p = .0054).

The fourth stress factor, which discusses the activity of the child, was most frequently cited by protective service investigators. Parents overreacted to crying, disobedience, hostility or some other behavior of the child in 91% of the cases.

AGENCY INVOLVEMENT

Most (95%) of the families in this group of confirmed abuse cases received some type of social services after investigation of the incident. However, few of them subsequently became involved with the court. In 77%, no juvenile court proceedings were initiated and there was no involvement with criminal court in 82%.

For those families who were referred to juvenile court, the most likely decision was for transfer of custody (47% of the court cases). Supervision of the family was ordered in 37 instances (19%). In only two incidents were parental rights terminated. Criminal court proceedings followed a similar path, with the more serious legal decisions occurring less often. Most of this court involvement terminated in the district attorney's office (57%). In only 14 cases (9%), the court had sentenced the abuser at the time of data collection.

No differences were found between boys and girls in the proportion of cases resulting in court action. However, abuse of younger children was more likely to result in such proceedings. In one-quarter of the cases of infant abuse, but only 13% of the teenage cases, such action was taken. Criminal court proceedings were instituted in 3% of the instances where young children were abused but less than 1% of those involving juveniles. Abusive mothers and fathers were equally likely to be referred to juvenile court, but thirteen of the fourteen abusers involved with criminal court were males.

Abuse resulted in placement of the child outside of the home for one-third of the sample (260 cases). 85 of them were subsequently returned to their home. One-third of the children who were placed went to foster homes, one-quarter moved to relative's homes, and 7% were institutionalized. Siblings were also removed from the home in 13% of the instances where the child had brothers and sisters (85 cases).

The decision to remove the child was not related to the gender of the child, but placement, like court action, was associated with the child's age. In contrast to findings on court referral, however, it was not infants but adolescents who were most likely to be removed. 40% of the teenagers, 25% of the latency-aged children and one-third of the infants were moved to alternative residential settings. Removal of siblings occurred most often when the abused child was not yet school age. 20% of the infants had siblings taken from the home, but this was done in only 10% of the cases involving older children.

Placement occurred much more often than the relatively minor form of abuse found in most instances would have led us to expect. The child was removed even when injuries sustained were relatively minor and he or she received no medical attention for them.

Results also suggest that boys and girls were dealt with in similar ways in terms of agency decision-making, at least insofar as removal from the home and court referrals are concerned. Mothers and fathers, too, were not differentially dealt with by the juvenile court. However, despite the fact that males did not injur children more severely than females, they were more likely to become involved in criminal court proceedings and to be sentenced as a result.

The most striking finding in terms of agency involvement with the family was that the age of the child had a consistent relationship with the type of decisions that were made. Abuse of young children in particular was more likely to lead to court action and to removal of siblings from the home. This may have occurred in consideration of the more serious nature of the injuries sustained by these children. Concern about the advisability of continued child-rearing by the parent and the desire to obtain some legal jurisdiction in the case are both more clearly evident when parents abuse children who are younger than six.

The age of the child was associated with agency decision-making in one other respect. Adolescents were most likely to be placed outside the home subsequent to abuse. Two out of every five children older than twelve are affected in this way. Here, however, it was not the severity of the injury that led to such actions on behalf of children. Unfortunately, the nature of the data does not provide clues to the rationale used for such decisions, although one may speculate that the adolescent's greater independence and desire to separate from the family may be factors taken into consideration when determining that these children are to be removed.

GENERAL CHARACTERISTICS OF ABUSE

We have previously defined four primary characteristics of abuse of special significance for development of hypotheses for the study: abusive parents hold unusually high expectations for their children; frequently, only one child in the family is abused; this child is an active participant in the abusive event; one abusive episode is frequently part of an ongoing pattern of abusive interaction between the parent and child. Data were available to examine the relevance of the last three of these factors for the sample under study.

Two measures were used to assess whether it is one child in the family who was the primary target for abuse. One question on the report form asked the protective service worker to note which children in the family had been previously maltreated. Although this information was missing in a large number of cases (almost 60%), the abuse child was the only one with an abuse history in half the remaining cases. In one-third, both the child and siblings were previously abused. A second question asked the worker to list the number of siblings of the child who have been previously abused. Again missing information was cited in large number of cases (57%). In the remaining incidents, no siblings were abused in 73%.

Several problems with these measures are evident. It is difficult to determine the meaning of the missing data, since there is no space provided on the form to note the child has no siblings and, for the first measure, no space to note that no prior abuse has occurred. The data from the two sources also do not match. 98 incidents of sibling abuse were cited using the second measure, but 168 were noted using the first. This information must, therefore, be interpreted with a great deal of caution. It suggests two possible patterns of abuse, one in which a single target was evident and a second in which violence was directed at a number of children in the family. Whether one child is singled out in other ways by parents (the most seriously abused, perceived as the most troublesome, etc.) is a question that must be examined in future research.

Evidence concerning the child's participation in abuse was provided by the protective service worker, who was asked to indicate whether the child's behavior was a stress factor of signficance just before the incident. As we have previously noted, abuse resulted from parental overreaction to such behavior in nine of ten cases. A second assessment of the child's role was provided by the coder who, after reading the description of the incident on the report form, was asked to indicate whether the abuse was victim precipitated. The coder found this to be true for 77% of the events. This judgment can, of course, be questioned, since it is based on a limited amount of information about cases. However, the consistency and size of the findings from two different sources are impressive. It does seem that the child plays an active role in interaction with the parent that results in abuse.

It has also been suggested that abuse is usually part of an ongoing pattern of interaction between parent and child, rather than an isolated, unrepeated incident. As only a rough indicator of the presence of this pattern, the report form indicates whether the child has been previously abused. Workers found this to be the case in only 35% of the incidents. Moreover, physical evidence of previous abuse was found only 30% of the time. Although lack of detailed knowledge of the history of parent-child interaction in the family threatens validity of these measures, they do suggest that the existence of an ongoing abusive relationship may not be the norm in most cases.

To summarize, the relevance of three major facts of abuse for families in this study has been assessed. One characteristic, suggesting that the child plays an active role in abusive events, was found relevant for cases examined here. A second characteristic, pointing to abuse of only one child in the family, was found applicable to at least half the families in the sample. However, the assumption that abusive behavior is part of a repetitive pattern of parent-child interaction was not found typical of most of the incidents studied.

REPRESENTATIVENESS OF THE SAMPLE

The sample was designed to include all confirmed cases of abuse in Wisconsin during 1974-1975 in which parents of the child were the abusers. In 1974-1975 there were 3655 cases of alleged abuse in the state. 1621 of these were unconfirmed, and 295 involved sexual abuse. The remaining 1739 incidents were perpetrated by a variety of individuals.

Parents mistreated the child in 74% of the total. Assuming they are abusers to the same extent in verified and unconfirmed cases, it is estimated that 1284 incidents of confirmed, non-sexual parental abuse occurred in the state during the study years. The sample of 830 cases is, therefore, two-thirds complete.

Conclusions drawn from the study are designed to apply to all true cases of child abuse perpetrated by parents. Assessment of the similarity between sample characteristics and other available data on the population provides evidence that can be used to determine generalizability of research results.

The sample will be compared with information from three other sources: published statistics on abuse in Wisconsin during 1974-1975 (Division of Family Services, no data-a, no date-b); a summary of abuse data for 1967-1976 in Wisconsin (Oghalai, 1977); and national data for 1976 published by the American Humane Association (1978). The first of these sources provides a more complete picture of abuse in the state during the study years. However, these data, as well as those provided in the ten-year summary, do not always differentiate between unconfirmed and verified incidents in the statistics compiled. The national study covers 31 states and three territories and cites only verified cases of abuse. However, in some areas, it does not differentiate between abuse and neglect incidents.

Table 3 summarizes material on the independent variables of the study from the three sources and the sample. Boys and girls were abused in each of the groups to approximately the same extent. Slightly more than half of the parents are abusive fathers in each of the four reports. The three Wisconsin surveys find that most of the abusers are natural parents of the child. National data

TABLE 3

COMPARISON OF SAMPLE DATA WITH OTHER INFORMATION ON ABUSIVE FAMILIES

	TYPE OF DATA					
	THE CHILD			THE PARENT		
DATA SOURCE	GENDER	AGE	GENDER×AGE	GENDER	AGE	TYPE
1974-1975 Wisconsin Abuse Cases (Division of Family Services, no date-a, no date-b) (N=3655)	45.7% Boys	Median age of 7	More Boys to age 10, more teenage girls	53% Males	52% Over 30	85.7% Natural Parents
1967-1976 Wisconsin Abuse Cases (Oghalai, no date) (N=9390)	47.9% Boys	Median age of 7	No data	54% Males	No data	85.1% Natural Parents
1977 National Abuse Cases (American Humane Association, no date)	46.0% Boys (N=18563)(N=18563)	Median age of 8	More boys to age 11, more girls (N=18563)	55% Males (N=13558)(N=50600)	56%* Over 30	No data
1974-1975 Sample Cases (N=830)	44.9% Boys	Median age of 9	More boys 1-10, more girls 13-17	59% Males	63.3% Over 30	83.3% Natural Parents

*Includes Neglect Cases

are not available for this statistic.

Both the parents and children in the sample are older than those included in the other studies. Alleged abused children in Wisconsin have a median age of seven; nationally, their average age is eight; children in the sample have a median age of nine. 52% of the parents were over 30 in Wisconsin during 1974-1975. This compares with 56% nationally and 63% in the sample.[1] All four data sources report that boys are over-represented among younger abused children, while adolescents are more likely to be girls.

No information is published in the Wisconsin reports on the economic position of the family. Analysis of the nationwide data suggests that, like the sample cases, abusive families tend to come from the poorer segments of the population. The median income of the parents, according to the American Humane Association (1978, p. 13), is $6886. 25% of the national families had incomes insufficient to meet their needs.

Based on these comparisons, the sample seems to be generally representative of abuse cases in the U. S. Children and parents are slightly older, however. Since the age of the child has differential relationships with a variety of factors associated with abuse, this fact should be kept in mind when assessing applicability of findings to abuse incidents in general.

To further check adequacy of the sample, descriptions of the incident and agency involvement with the family were also compared.

As Table 4 points out, Wisconsin reports tend to include more incidents in which injuries are minor. The sample underrepresents the more serious types of abuse situations. Protective service workers in Wisconsin are also more likely to provide social services to the family than are those in other states. In over 90% of the Wisconsin cases services were made available, while this occurred in only half of the cases nationally.[2]

No national information is available on the number of cases referred to court or the children removed from home as a result of abuse. The ten-year survey in Wisconsin also omits these data. Published Wisconsin statistics for 1974-1975 report fewer children placed (28%) than in the sample (36%). This is under-

TABLE 4
COMPARISON OF SAMPLE DATA WITH OTHER INFORMATION ON ABUSE INCIDENTS

	THE INCIDENT			TYPE OF DATA — AGENCY INVOLVEMENT			
DATA SOURCE	INJURY	MEDICAL ATTENTION	REPORTER	SERVICES	JUVENILE COURT	CRIMINAL COURT	PLACEMENT
1974-1975 Wisconsin Abuse Cases (Division of Family Services, no data-a, no date-b	81.8%* Cuts, Bruises, Welts (N=1719)	No data	49.8% Professionals (N=3655)	Received by 94%* (N=2067)	24.5%* referred (N=2034)	31.8%* referred (N=2034)	27.8% placed (N=3655)
1967-1976 Wisconsin Abuse Cases (Oghalai, no date)	77.7%* Cuts, Bruises, Welts (N=6140)	No data	54.5% Professionals (N=9390)	No data	No data	No data	No data
1977 National Abuse Cases (American Humane Association, no date)	63.4% Cuts, Bruises Welts (N=18500)	65% No Treatment 10% Hospitalized (N=10213)	44.4%** Professionals (N=99071)	Received by 53.6%** (N=32657)	No data	No data	No data
1974-1975 Sample Cases (N=830)	84.9% Cuts, Bruises, Welts	60.6% No treatment 5.7% Hospitalized	57.7% Professionals	Received by 94.9%	23.5% referred	18.9% referred	35.7% placed

* Valid Cases only
** Includes Neglect Cases

standable since, in the unverified cases included in the statewide report, children should be less likely to be removed.

One would expect that approximately the same percentage of cases result in court action in both the published Wisconsin report and in the sample, since the Wisconsin statistics do distinguish here between validated and unconfirmed cases. This does occur in the case of juvenile court referrals. However, this is not true for criminal court proceedings. In the sample, fewer cases (19%) were involved with this court than with the juvenile court. In the 1974-1975 state data, the opposite occurs. More cases (32%) were referred to the district attorney for criminal prosecution than were sent to juvenile authorities.

This statistic suggests an explanation for some of the missing sample cases. If abusive families are involved in criminal court proceedings, their records might be removed from the files for use in court. Infant abuse records would also be missing more frequently since their parents are more likely to be referred to this court than are those of older children. It is difficult to determine the effect of this factor on generalizability of results except to, again, point out that the sample may under-represent the more serious abuse situations in which young children are too severely disciplined by their parents.

After comparing sample characteristics with those described in other published abuse reports, it appears that sample cases are, for the most part, representative of all reported incidents of parental abuse. However, results of this study are most appropriately applied to a population of cases in which children are slightly older and somewhat less seriously injured than abused children nationwide.

FOOTNOTES

[1]Note, however, that the national data include neglect cases, in which mothers are more likely to be the perpetrators. Mothers, in that study, also tend to be younger than fathers. Thus,

if only abuse cases were considered, there would probably be a larger number of parents 30 or older.

[2]Note, however, that these national cases include neglect as well as abuse. Services may be provided less often in neglect situations, thereby lowering the overall proportion of cases in which social services are provided.

CHAPTER V

RESULTS

Three of the hypotheses outlined in Chapter II examine the behaviors of boys and girls that precipitate abuse. Four additional hypotheses predict that other factors (age of the child, gender of the parent, socio-economic status of the family) affect this basic relationship. Results of the study relative to these predictions are the subject of this chapter.

BEHAVIOR OF BOYS AND GIRLS IN ABUSIVE SITUATIONS

Nine behavior categories were studied in this research. These behaviors were exhibited by children and, it has been argued, served as precipitating factors in abuse situations. Actions on the part of the child do not "cause" abuse, but they do serve as one source of stimuli to which parents react when they maltreat boys and girls.

The frequency with which these behaviors were found in the sample is reported in Table 5. Aggression and defiance were the most prevalent behaviors. Children displayed aggression in one-fifth of the cases. Most of this activity was verbal in form (79%), and three-quarters of these acts had as a target an adult rather than a child (Table 6). Defiant behavior was also found in one of every five incidents examined. Most of this behavior in-

TABLE 5
BEHAVIORS OF CHILDREN IN ABUSE SITUATIONS

BEHAVIOR CATEGORY	FREQUENCY	PERCENT*
Aggression	156	18.8%
Active Behaviors	37	4.5%
Defiance	166	20.0%
Expression of Emotional Upset	69	8.3%
Achievement-Related Behaviors	51	6.1%
Social Behaviors	46	5.5%
Behaviors Reflecting on Personal Appearance	15	1.8%
Performance of Household Tasks	61	7.3%
Sex-Related Behaviors	38	4.6%
TOTAL	830	--------

*Note: More than one behavior may appear in one abuse case. Categories are overlapping and are not additive.

TABLE 6
INTENSITY LEVEL OF CHILDREN'S BEHAVIORS

BEHAVIOR CATEGORY	INTENSITY LEVEL	FREQUENCY	PERCENT
	High:Physical at Adults	19	12.2%
	Moderate: Verbal at Adults	98	62.8%
Aggression	Moderate:Physical at Peers	11	7.1%
	Low:Verbal at Peers	25	16.0%
	Unclassified	3	1.9%
	TOTAL	156	100.0%
	674 Cases: Behavior Not Present		
	High .	24	64.9%
Active	Moderate	9	24.3%
Behaviors	Low	4	10.8%
	TOTAL	37	100.0%
	793 Cases: Behavior Not Present		
	High	30	18.1%
Defiance	Moderate	135	81.3%
	Unclassified	1	.6%
	TOTAL	166	100.0%
	664 Cases: Behavior Not Present		
	High	17	24.6%
Expression of	Moderate	17	24.6%
Emotional Upset	Unclassified	35	50.7%
	TOTAL	69	100.0%
	761 Cases: Behavior Not Present		

volved failure of the child to obey after being given only one command to do so. Evidence of prolonged refusal to respond to parental commands was found in only 30 cases.

Seven types of behavior appeared in less than ten percent of the cases. Expression of emotional upset by the child triggered abuse in 69 instances. In half of these situations, insufficient data were available to assess the intensity level of the behavior. Of the 34 remaining cases, half involved persistent crying, worrying or other forms of emotional upset, while half described such behavior but did not indicate any persistence (Table 6).

Behaviors associated with performance of household tasks served as stimuli in abuse events only 61 times. In fifty of these cases, housekeeping tasks (picking up toys, sweeping floors, washing dishes, etc.) were at issue. In nine incidents, babysitting chores were noted. Achievement-related behaviors of the child served as precipitating factors in abuse in only 51 cases, and in 49 of these educational problems were discussed. The child was failing academically, was not attending school or was misbehaving in the classroom. Sociable behaviors were at issue in 46 cases. In 39, the child was described as unable to relate to others or get along with them generally. Deficits in social manners were noted in only seven instances.

The remaining categories were located in less than five percent of the sample. In contrast to aggressive and defiant behavior, which tended to be moderate in intensity level, active behaviors were more likely to trigger abuse when they were severe and persistent (24 cases). In nine instances the behavior was moderate in intensity, while underactivity or bodily lethargy was present only four times. In 27 of the 38 sex-related behavioral events, dating issues were the source of parent-child conflict. Very few cases concerned sex play, or conflict over intercourse or pregnancy. In one case the child was described as "too sexy" in her behavior towards the parent. Behavioral issues reflecting on personal appearance of the child appeared rarely (15 cases).

Procedures used to measure these dependent variables allowed for the presence of more than one of them during an abuse event. Because of this, it is possible that they cluster together into a number of subgroups. Examination of intercorrelations (Appendix B, Table 6) suggest that this is not the case. The most frequently occurring of the categories, aggression and defiance, do not occur in the same situations ($r = -.0478$), although each is associated with other behaviors. Aggression correlates with sociability ($r = .1126$) and negatively with emotional upset ($r = -.1337$). Defiance is associated with performance of household tasks ($r = .1708$) and personal appearance items ($r = .1131$). It is negatively correlated with achievement-related issues ($r = -.0903$). None of these associations is particularly strong. The highest correlation, between defiance and performance of household tasks, explains only 3% of the variance in each variable. Failure to find strong associations suggests that each of the dependent variables may be considered a distinct type of activity to be examined in tests of the hypotheses.

GENDER OF THE CHILD AND BEHAVIORS PRECIPITATING ABUSE

Hypothesis one predicts that children of a particular gender are more likely to be abused when engaged in gender-consistent behaviors than are children of the opposite gender. Boys will be abused when engaged in aggressive, active, defiant or achievement-related behaviors, girls when expressing emotional upset, sociable behaviors or those associated with personal appearance or performance of household tasks. Table 7 contains results relative to these predictions.

Significant differences between boys and girls were found for two of the categories. As predicted, boys were more likely to engage in active behaviors. They were involved in such situations more than three times as often as girls. Girls were twice as likely to engage in aggressive activities. However, this finding contrasts with our prediction that boys would be more aggressive.

In a third category, gender differences were suggestive. Girls were involved in issues concerning performance of household tasks almost twice as often as boys. In each of the five remaining behavioral groups, no significant differences were found. Boys

TABLE 8
GENDER OF CHILD AND SEX-RELATED BEHAVIOR

SEX-RELATED BEHAVIOR	GENDER OF CHILD	
	MALE	FEMALE
Present	.3%	8.1%
	(1)	(37)
Absent	99.7%	91.9%
	(372)	(418)
TOTAL	100.0%	100.0%
	(373)	(455)

Chi square = 27.18, d.f. = 1, p = .0000
N = 828

CHAPTER I

LIFE ON THE STREETS

Prostitution is personally dangerous and destructive in terms of the self-alienation and proclivity for violence inherent in the activity. Though many youth first experience some form of prostitution at home, most join the ranks of over one million serious runaways each year. They act on a healthy impulse for survival by escaping home situations that include neglect, divorce, physical abuse and incest. There is no reliable estimate of the number of juveniles engaged in prostitution. A former treatment center in Minneapolis served 200 youth in a two year period and estimated that at any given time, approximately 2,300 females and possibly 200 male children were active on the streets.

Stereotypically, the youth arrives in an alien city with no resources for living. Their introduction to prostitution occurs through initial contact with a customer. A man drives up to them on the street or picks them up hitchhiking. He offers money to "help them out." The deed in exchange is sexual. The youth is seldom surprised since many have experimented with sex for money prior to leaving their home which contributed to the dynamics that allow this behavior to become an option. Frequently, the female youth recalls a childhood label of whore or slut pronounced by a significant family

study of his or her actions during abusive episodes is established by these findings. However, the utility of conceptualizing these differences along gender-consistent lines is brought into serious questions by the results.

GENDER OF THE CHILD AND INTENSITY LEVEL OF BEHAVIORS

Hypothesis two predicts that gender differences also exist in terms of the intensity levels of behaviors exhibited during abusive events. When a particular behavior is consistent for children of one gender but inconsistent for those of the opposite gender, the gender-consistent group will engage in more extreme forms of the behavior. Boys are expected to be involved in more intense forms of aggression, activity and defiance, girls in more extreme forms of emotional upset. Results relative to this hypothesis are shown in Table 9.

Physical aggression directed at adults, the most extreme form of this behavior examined in this study, occurred in one out of every five situations where boys were aggressive but only one in ten of the girls incidents. Boys were also four times as likely to

TABLE 9

GENDER OF CHILD AND INTENSITY LEVEL OF BEHAVIOR

| BEHAVIOR CATEGORY | INTENSITY LEVEL | GENDER OF CHILD | |
		MALE	FEMALE
Aggression	High: Physical, Adults	19.0% (8)	9.9% (11)
	Moderate: Verbal, Adults	47.6% (20)	70.3% (78)
	Moderate: Physical, Peers	16.7% (7)	3.6% (4)
	Low: Verbal, Peers	16.7% (7)	16.2% (18)

Chi square = 11.73, d.f. = 3, p = .0084
N= 153

	INTENSITY LEVEL	MALE	FEMALE
Active Behaviors	High	66.7% (18)	60.0% (6)
	Moderate	22.2% (6)	30.0% (3)
	Low	11.1% (3)	10.0% (1)

N. S.
N = 37

	INTENSITY LEVEL	MALE	FEMALE
Defiance	High	20.0% (15)	16.7% (15)
	Moderate	80.0% (60)	83.3% (75)

N. S.
N = 165

	INTENSITY LEVEL	MALE	FEMALE
Expression of Emotional Upset	High	53.8% (7)	47.6% (10)
	Moderate	46.2% (6)	52.4% (11)

N. S.
N = 34

be physically aggressive with peers. Girls were more likely to be verbally abusive toward adults. 70% of these aggressive acts were of this type. Reexamining these results along simpler physical-verbal dimensions (Table 10), it is clear that boys were more likely to be physically aggressive, girls to be verbally aggressive. For this particular behavioral area, results were in the direction predicted by the hypothesis.

TABLE 10
GENDER OF CHILD AND INTENSITY
OF AGGRESSIVE BEHAVIOR

INTENSITY OF AGGRESSIVE BEHAVIOR	GENDER OF CHILD	
	MALE	FEMALE
High: Physical	35.7%	13.5%
	(15)	(15)
Moderate: Verbal	64.3%	86.5%
	(27)	(96)
TOTAL	100.0%	100.0%
	(42)	(111)

Chi square = 8.17, d.f. = 1, p = .0043
N = 153

However, no differences in intensity level were found for the other categories studied. While the prediction explains gender differences for one particular activity, there was no general tendency for boys and girls to exhibit behaviors of varying intensity levels, depending upon gender-consistency or -inconsistency of their actions. As an overall explanation for differences between male and female children, the hypothesis is rejected.

IMPACT OF SECONDARY INDEPENDENT VARIABLES

Remaining hypotheses outline the impact of selected variables on the basic relationship between gender of the child and behavior precipitating abuse. These variables are expected to clarify the conditions under which boys and girls engage in the various behaviors studied. Three secondary independent variables are considered here: age of the child, gender of the parent, and social class status of the family.

AGE OF THE CHILD

Children of all ages are represented in the sample. For the purposes of data analysis, age has been divided into three groups: birth through five years (infancy), six through twelve (latency), and thirteen to seventeen (adolescence). Slightly less than one-third of the children are infants, while 36% are in each of the other age groups.

There were significant differences among the age levels in the extent they engaged in many of the behaviors studied (Appendix B, Table 7). In four categories, age and activity were positively correlated. One-third of the adolescent cases involved aggressive behavior, while only 8% of the infant cases did so. For 12% of the adolescents and only 2% of children younger than six, performance of household tasks was at issue. Achievement-related and sociable behaviors served as stimuli for abuse much more frequently for teenagers.

For a fifth category, that focusing on sex-linked issues, cases almost exclusively involved children in their teens. For expression of emotional upset, the opposite occurred. It was evident in one-quarter of the infant cases but less than 2% of those involving older children.

In only three areas were there no distinctive differences among the groups. Children of all ages exhibited defiance, active behaviors, and those reflecting on personal appearance in approximately equal proportions. Maturity level is, therefore, a significant factor in understanding activities of abused children. Defiance is the only behavior present in a significant number of cases that did not vary with the age of the child.

Hypothesis four predicts that, with increased age, gender differences will emerge more strongly. Age did affect the relationship between gender and behavior for three of the four behavior categories studied under this hypothesis.

When aggression was examined, a progressive increase in expression of the behavior with increased age was found for both boys and girls (Table 11).

TABLE 11
AGE AND GENDER OF CHILD ASSOCIATED WITH
AGGRESSIVE BEHAVIOR

GENDER OF CHILD	AGE OF CHILD			CONTROL FOR GENDER
	INFANCY	LATENCY	ADOLESCENCE	
Male	8.9%	9.8%	25.4%	Chi square =
	(12)	(15)	(18)	13.317, d.f. = 2,
				p = .0013, N=359
Female	7.1%	16.9%	38.2%	Chi square =
	(7)	(22)	(81)	40.913, d.f. = 2,
				p = .0000, N=440
Control for Age	N.S.	N.S.	N.S.	

Adolescent boys were almost three times as likely as infants to behave in this way; teenage girls were more than five times as likely to display such behavior than very young girls. However, when individual age categories were studied, the gender differences tended to become less, not more distinct. Male and female infants were aggressive in approximately the same proportion, and there was a non-significant difference between the proportion of adolescent boys (25%) and girls (38%) in their expression of this behavior.

Examination of partial correlations suggests that gender of the child still had some, albeit slight, importance, even when controlling for age of the child ($r_{ab.c}$ = -.0847, Appendix B, Table 8). However, age of the child was more highly correlated with the behavior (r = -.2897), and this persisted when controlling for gender of the child ($r_{ab.c}$ = -.2599). Age, therefore, is a more important determinant of expression of aggressive behavior than is gender.

In another category, performance of household tasks, age also had an impact on expression of the behavior, but only for girls. While 2% of infant girls were abused for issues surrounding household duties, 15% of adolescent girls were so involved (Table 12). These age differences were not found for boys. Within any one age category, there were no significant differences between boys and girls in expression of this behavior. Therefore, age did not clarify variations between male and female children, as the hypothesis predicts. Instead, gender of the child had a differential impact on age effects. Only when the child was a girl was increased evidence of the behavior found with increased maturity.

TABLE 12
AGE AND GENDER OF CHILD ASSOCIATED WITH
PERFORMANCE OF HOUSEHOLD TASKS

| GENDER OF CHILD | AGE OF CHILD | | | CONTROL FOR GENDER |
	INFANCY	LATENCY	ADOLESCENCE	
Male	2.2%	6.5%	5.6%	N.S.
	(3)	(10)	(4)	
Female	2.0%	6.9%	14.6%	Chi square =
	(2)	(9)	(31)	13.757, d.f. = 2,
				p = .0010, N=440
Control for Age	N.S.	N.S.	N.S.	

Examining sex-related behaviors, age and gender of the child combined to produce one particular category (adolescent girls) who were abused when engaging in this type of activity. It is only in adolescence that the boy-girl differences in its expression were significant. No teenage boys and 31 of the girls were abused for this behavior (Table 13). Only five girls younger than thirteen exhibited it, while for boys, only one case was found in the entire sample. As the hypothesis predicts, data in this case points to the emergence of gender differences in adolescence.

TABLE 13
AGE AND GENDER OF CHILD ASSOCIATED WITH
SEX-RELATED BEHAVIORS

GENDER OF CHILD	AGE OF CHILD			CONTROL FOR GENDER
	INFANCY	LATENCY	ADOLESCENCE	
Male	.7%	0.0%	0.0%	N.S.
	(1)	(0)	(0)	
Female	2.0%	2.3%	14.6%	Chi square =
	(2)	(3)	(31)	22.597, d.f. = 2,
				p = .0000, N=440
Control for Age	N.S.	N.S.	Chi square = 10.208, d.f. = 1 p = .0014, N=283	

Age effects were examined for one other category — active behaviors. Age did not have any appreciable impact on expression of this behavior. Analysis of the three different age groups points to no significant gender differences within any of them.

Examining the validity of hypothesis four based on results obtained, it is clear that modification of this hypothesis is required. For certain types of actions (sex-related behavior), the hypothesis has validity and should not be rejected. However, in other instances, age has an effect different from that outlined in the hypothesis. In the case of active behavior, age has no impact; for performance of household tasks, age differences are found only for girls; with aggression, it proves of overriding importance, suggesting gender effects are largely spurious. Age, gender and particular types of behavior are associated in complex and changeable ways, depending upon the particular type of activity studied.

Although the child's age is a factor of some significance in under-standing the actions of children during abuse events, the relation-ship between age and this behavior suggested by hypothesis four is too simplistic to fully explain results obtained in this research.

GENDER OF THE PARENT

There were slightly more male than female abusers in the sample. Almost all of them were the child's natural parents. In contrast to results obtained when various behaviors were examined relative to the age of the child, only one significant difference emerged between male and female abusers in the type of child's behavior to which they responded. While 7% of the mothers abused children who were active, only 3% of the fathers did so. These findings suggest that, in general, mothers and fathers were reacting to similar types of behavioral stimuli in abuse situations, at least insofar as the specific types of categories included in this research are concerned.

Hypothesis five predicts that for male abusers, gender differ-ences in behavior between boys and girls will become more dis-tinct, while for mothers this gender difference becomes less clear-cut. In the case of two of the four behavior categories studied, fathers differentiated between boys and girls in their response to the behavior, while mothers did not. Fathers abused no boys for sex-related behaviors, but in 11% of the instances where they abused daughters, such behavior was present (Table 14). Fathers, then, were more likely to abuse girls than boys for such behavior, while mothers did not make this gender-related distinction.

A similar pattern of results were obtained when behaviors concerning performance of household tasks were studied, al-though results here are only suggestive (Table 15).

Hypothesis five has validity in some, but not all, circum-stances analyzed in this research. For two types of behavior (per-formance of household tasks, sex-related behaviors), fathers were more likely than mothers to differentially abuse boys and girls. For other behaviors, however, this was not the case. When children engaged in active or aggressive behavior, both parents were more

TABLE 14
GENDER OF ABUSER AND CHILD ASSOCIATED WITH
SEX-RELATED BEHAVIORS

| GENDER OF CHILD | GENDER OF ABUSER | | CONTROL FOR GENDER OF CHILD |
	MALE	FEMALE	
Male	0.0% (0)	.7% (1)	N.S.
Female	10.7% (29)	4.3% (8)	Chi square = 5.222, d.f. = 1, p = .0223, N=455
Control for Gender of Abuser	Chi square = 23.331, d.f. = 1, p = .0000, N=491	N.S.	

TABLE 15
GENDER OF ABUSER AND CHILD ASSOCIATED WITH
PERFORMANCE OF HOUSEHOLD TASKS

| GENDER OF CHILD | GENDER OF ABUSER | | CONTROL FOR GENDER OF CHILD |
	MALE	FEMALE	
Male	4.5% (10)	5.3% (8)	N.S.
Female	10.4% (28)	8.1% (15)	N.S.
Control for Gender of Abuser	Chi square = 5.026, d.f. = 1, p = .0250, N-491	N.S.	

likely to abuse children of one gender than of the other. In these instances, the hypothesis must be rejected.

Hypothesis six predicts that parents who are of the same gender as the child are more likely to abuse that child for a particular behavior than are parents of the opposite gender. To test this hypothesis, parents and children were initially distinguished along same-gender (mother-daughter, father-son) versus cross-gender (mother-son, father-daughter) lines. The proportion of cases in which precipitating behaviors were present for each group was then studied (Table 16). Only in the case of sex-related behaviors were there significant differences between the same gender and cross-gender groups. However, results are in a direction opposite to that predicted by the hypothesis. Abuse for such behavior is more likely to occur in cross-gender situations.

TABLE 16
COMBINED GENDER OF ABUSER AND CHILD ASSOCIATED
WITH BEHAVIORS OF CHILD

	ABUSER AND CHILD		
BEHAVIOR CATEGORY	SAME GENDER	OPPOSITE GENDER	SIGNIFICANCE LEVEL
Aggression	17.7% (72)	19.9% (84)	N.S.
Active Behaviors	4.7% (19)	4.3% (18)	N.S.
Performance of Household Tasks	6.2% (25)	8.5% (36)	N.S.
Sex-Related Behaviors	2.0% (8)	7.1% (30)	Chi square = 11.33, d.f. = 1, p = .0008, N=828

Examination of data on sex-related behavior from Table 14 raises questions concerning this conclusion. Father-daughter incidents provided 29 of the 30 cases in the cross-gender category. Therefore, it is not cross-gender interaction but father-daughter interaction that produces abuse for sex-related behaviors. Although complex relationships between the gender of parent and child may exist, a simple cross-gender/same-gender distinction is not adequate for understanding these relationships. Hypothesis six is, therefore, rejected.

Interaction effects of gender of the parent and child should be noted in one other category. These effects are masked by use of the cross-gender/same-gender distinction. Data suggest that mothers were more likely to abuse sons and fathers to abuse daughters for active behavior. Examination of partial correlations clarified the impact of gender of the parent here. Boys were more likely to be abused for such behavior than girls (r = .1214), even when controlling for gender of the parent ($r_{ab.c}$ = .1220; Appendix B, Table 8). However, mothers were also more likely than fathers to abuse children for such behavior (r = -.1061), even when controlling for gender of the child ($r_{ab.c}$ = -.1068). Both mothers and fathers were more likely to abuse boys for such behavior, but mothers in particular were likely to respond abusively to sons in such situations. (Note that the effects of gender of the parent here are only suggestive.)

In summary, the parent's gender is an important factor differentiating between the behavior of boys and girls in abuse situations. Results are similar to those cited when age of the child was considered. It is only when certain types of behavior are studied (sex-related and active behavior) and only under certain circumstances that the impact of the parent's sex can be seen. Fathers are more likely than mothers to differentiate between boys and girls when sex-related behaviors and those relating to performance of household tasks are involved. Fathers and daughters are most likely to be in conflict over sex-related issues. Mothers and fathers are both more likely to abuse boys for exhibiting active behaviors, although mothers are particularly prone to do so. The hypotheses considered here do not provide adequate guidelines for understanding these results. They are in need of revision.

SOCIO-ECONOMIC STATUS OF THE FAMILY AND THE ABUSER

As we have reported in Chapter IV, the sample does not include a range of social class groups. Most of the cases come from lower class families. This fact creates difficulties when attempting to assess the behavior of boys and girls from various socio-economic groups. The small number of such children from upper status groups produces results that make conclusions concerning status effects risky. Small sample sizes in higher level groups make it unlikely that significant differences between boys and girls will be obtained, while large sample sizes in lower class groups may produce significant results even though differences between the behavior of boys and girls are slight.

Two primary measures of socio-economic status were used. Family social class measures were based on weighted scores assigned to occupational and educational levels of the primary parent for whom data was available (492 fathers and 141 mothers). Social class was not associated with expression of the various behaviors except on one instance. Parents in upper class families were more likely to abuse children when sociable behaviors are at issue than were those from middle and lower class homes. In 5% of the lower class families and one-quarter of the upper class homes (Classes I-II), this behavior served as a precipitating factor for abuse (Chi square = 13.153, df = 4, p = .0106).

The second primary measure assesses the occupation of the parent who actually abused the child. More than one-fifth of these adults (23%) were unskilled laborers. Another 23% were home-makers (all but one of these being mothers). Very few of these adults (8%) were from professional or semi-professional occupations. Occupation of the abuser was not associated with the type of behavior children display during abusive events. Parents from the various occupational groups responded to similar types of behavior when they maltreated children.

Hypothesis seven predicts that socio-economic status is related to gender differences in precipitating behaviors. In lower socio-economic groups, these gender differences are expected to be more evident than in families from higher social class groups.

When aggressive behavior is considered, significant differences between boys and girls were found only in the two lowest class groups. In lower middle class families, 28% of the girls and only 8% of the boys were abused for aggression. 24% of the girls and 12% of the boys in lower class homes were abused when acting aggressively. However, similar but nonsignificant gender differences were found for upper class groups as well. In those homes, half of the girls but none of the boys were abused when acting aggressively. These findings suggest that consistent social class differences do not exist for this behavior.

Analysis of results for the three remaining behavioral groups used to test hypothesis seven points to the same conclusion.

Focusing on active behaviors, none of the children in Classes I-III were abused for such behavior. Significant differences in the proportion of cases involving such activity were found for boys and girls from lower middle class homes. For 12% of the boys and only 1% of the girls from such families this behavior precipitated abuse. Significant differences were not found in the lower class sample. Assessment using partial correlations suggests no overall effect of social class on the degree male and female children are involved in such behavior.

When performance of household tasks was examined, it was found that no children from upper or upper middle class families displayed it. No significant differences between boys and girls were found for any social class group studied, although gender differences for the lowest class were suggestive.

Finally, evaluation of the effect of social class on involvement of boys and girls in sex-related behaviors revealed significant gender differences in the lowest social class. However, the lack of similar findings in other class groups was due to smaller sample sizes found in those groups. While gender of the child was correlated with expression of sex-related behavior in abuse situations ($r = -.1870$), control for social class did not alter this relationship ($r_{ab.c} = -.1859$; Appendix B, Table 8).

In general, then, there are no significant differences between lower and higher social class levels in the behavior of boys and girls during abuse episodes. With family social class used as a measure of socio-economic status, the hypothesis is rejected.

Use of occupation of the abusive parent as a measure of socio-economic status produced no significant differences between boys and girls in expression of aggression or active behavior within any of the occupational groups. Examining performance of household tasks, significant differences between boys and girls were found only for parents from the unskilled occupational category. Failure to find significant differences in higher status groups is, again, an artifact of the small sample sizes in these groups, since they showed a similar but non-significant tendency to abuse girls more often for this behavior. The same results were obtained when sex-related behaviors were studied. Abusive parents from lower status occupations were not consistently more likely to abuse girls for sex-related issues, as the hypothesis predicts.

Using two measures of socio-economic status and four measures for behavior of children, results proved singularly unproductive in finding significant differences in the behavior of boys and girls between higher and lower status groups. Hypothesis seven is rejected.

SUMMARY

Findings of the study are depicted in Figure 4. Analysis of these results suggests the importance of consideration of the child's gender for understanding the behavior of children in abuse situations. The differential impact of the age of the child and the gender of the parent in predicting the behavior of boys and girls have also been shown. Of the various independent variables considered, only socio-economic status had no significant effect on the relationship between gender of the child and the presence of these behaviors.

Despite these findings, hypotheses outlined for the study did not prove adequate. The first five hypotheses provided explanations for some specific behavioral differences between male and female children but were rejected when other behavioral data were considered. Some of the results were in a direction opposite to that predicted by these hypotheses. These five predictions are, therefore, in need of modification and specification of conditions under which they appear to be valid.

Two hypotheses do not prove helpful in understanding behavior of boys and girls in abusive interaction with parents. No significant same-gender/opposite-gender effects on behavior were observed (hypothesis six), and no differential social class effects were discovered (hypothesis seven). These hypotheses are rejected.

A general assessment of the complex relationships among gender of the parent and child, age of the child and behaviors precipitating abuse is provided in the following chapter.

FIGURE 4
SUMMARY OF RESULTS

Behavior Category	INDEPENDENT VARIABLES						
	Gender	Age	Gender By Age	Abuser	Gender by Abuser	SES	Gender By SES
Aggression	Girls More; Boys more intense	Older more	Older girls more - Age more important				
Active Behaviors	Boys more		✕		✕		✕
Defiance			✕		✕		✕
Expression of Emotional Upset		Only infants	✕	Mothers more	✕		✕
Achievement-related Behaviors		Older more	✕		Mothers and Boys more		✕
Sociable Behaviors		Older more	✕		✕		✕
Behaviors Reflecting on Personal Appearance			✕		✕		✕
Performance of Household Tasks	Girls More	Older More	Older more Only for girls		Fathers and Girls more		
Sex-Related Behaviors	Girls More	Older More	Mostly teen-age Girls		Fathers and Girls more		

Blank: No significant results in this Category

Category Crossed Out: Analysis not done in this Category

90

CHAPTER VI

DISCUSSION

Examination of the importance of study results for enriched understanding of the parameters and dynamics of abuse is the task dealt with in this chapter. Findings of the study will be discussed on two levels. Description of the nature of the sample and tests of hypotheses have suggested some key characteristics of abuse that require reemphasis here. Under the heading "Significant Findings," delineation of these characteristics provides information concerning the structure of abusive events.

This research has also considered interaction between parent and child that results in abusive behavior of adults in the family. The theoretical orientation used to develop hypotheses attempted to outline some of the interactive dynamics that may occur. Although assumptions and theoretical postulates could not be tested using the simple survey design required for this research, results do suggest some revisions in this theoretical orientation that should prove useful in future attempts to examine abuse events. This is the second topic of the chapter.

SIGNIFICANT FINDINGS

Major findings of the study are summarized in the following statements:

Children play an active role in abusive events. This study was based on the premise that interaction between the abusive parent and the child provides primary data for understanding dynamics of abuse. Findings of this study provide support for this premise. In over 90% of the 828 incidents examined, the behavior of the child in the situation was cited by the protective service worker as a major stress factor immediately preceding parental abusive behavior. Moreover, this factor was cited much more frequently than other potential sources of stress (arguments and fights in the family, use of drugs or alcohol by parents, family breakup or job loss). Data on the abuse reporting forms describing the incident consistently cited some behavior of the child to which parents were responding.

These data do not suggest that children "cause" abuse. However, they do strongly indicate that an adequate assessment of such behavior requires consideration of the role played by the child as well as that of the adult. Further analysis from a systems perspective is needed, a viewpoint that has been used extensively in the family therapy field but infrequently when examining the nature of abuse.

The type of role children play in abuse events varies, depending upon such basic characteristics as their age and gender. No child, whether a boy or girl, an infant or adolescent, is immune from abuse. In this study, approximately equal numbers of maltreated children were males and females, preschoolers and teenagers. However, knowledge of their age and gender does provide indications of some circumstances in which their conflict with parents is likely to result in excessive, harmful disciplining.

Parents tend to avoid abusing their adolescent sons and young daughters. This study echoes results of other research in its finding that boys younger than ten and girls who are adolescents are most likely to be targets for such parental behavior. Consideration of the age and gender of the child also provides clues concerning some potentially explosive problem areas that may escalate into abuse. The most clearcut patterns emerge for adolescent girls. They are especially prone to maltreatment if they are verbally or physically aggressive. More than one of every three adolescent girls in the sample were abused for such behavior. Daughters of this age are also more likely to be in conflict with parents over sex-related issues. Although a much smaller percentage of the children in the study engaged in such activity when it was at issue, it was almost invariably a female teenager who displayed it.

Unlike the girls, boys of different ages do not engage in distinctly different types of precipitating behaviors. They are, however, more likely than girls to be abused when being over-active or physically aggressive towards peers or adults.

Behaviors also differ in their potential for eliciting abuse, depending upon the age of the child. For younger children, crying seems to be a likely precipitant. As children grow older, a variety of issues — aggression, achievement, sociability and performance of household tasks — become increasingly salient as factors in the situation. Sex-related behaviors usually play a role in abuse only when children are adolescents.

One cautionary note must be added here. All behaviors of the children were not examined in this study. Only nine selected categories were considered. Some of them (aggression, defiance) proved to be frequent precursers of abuse, while others (sex-related issues, active behavior) rarely occurred. In this discussion we are not defining the types of behavior most likely to lead to maltreatment. Instead, among the limited number of behavior groups studied, knowledge of the gender and age of the child proves helpful in pointing out which of them has a higher poten-tial for eliciting abuse.

Male and female parents tend to react abusively to different types of children's behaviors. Results of this survey indicate that abusive parents are *not* usually mothers. Approximately three out of every five abusers in the sample were males.

Knowledge of the gender of the parent does suggest some particular behaviors of the child likely to be present in the abuse event although the relationship between these two variables is complex. Neither fathers nor mothers are more stringent in their enforcement of gender-related standards through the use of physical punishment. However, mothers do seem to find overactive behavior displayed by their sons more problematic than fathers do. Fathers, in turn, are more likely to become involved in conflict with their daughters over performance of household tasks and they are the only parents who abuse adolescent daughters when sex-related behavior is at issue. While all abusive parents seem to have problems controlling their disciplinary behavior when children behave aggressively or defiantly, mothers may require additional assistance in coping with their sons' active behavior, fathers in handling household chores and dating issues with their teenage daughters.

The protective service worker in a public welfare agency handles selected abuse cases. The data also point out the special nature of abuse cases handled by public protective service agencies who are generally responsible for investigation of suspected cases of mistreatment of children. Middle and upper class parents were conspicuous for their absence from the rolls of confirmed abusers in Wisconsin. They comprised only 10% of the sample.

Protective service workers are, therefore, mainly responsible for treating families who struggle under twin burdens posed by poverty and inadequate child-rearing techniques. These parents must grapple with difficulties inherent in poverty situations, including substandard housing, inadequate finances to properly feed and clothe family members, and limited educational resources that operate to keep members in this state. It is questionable whether workers can help parents raise their children in a more acceptable fashion without also tackling the especially difficult problems that result from and perpetuate their low standard of living.

At the same time that these cases are selective in terms of socio-economic status of the family, they also differ from incidents of abuse investigated in hospital settings. Hospitalized children tend to be younger and more severely injured. Many children referred for protective services sustain only minor injuries, and they are as likely to be adolescents as infants. The protective service worker must, therefore, be prepared to help families facing a wider variety of child-rearing dilemmas. They must be adept in coping with parenting problems which vary in seriousness and persistence. Demands on these workers are, indeed, heavy, for they must possess both investigative and treatment skills that enable them to help families in diverse situations while adjusting their expectations and adapting their skills to the limitations posed by poverty and low social standing in the community.

ASSESSMENT OF THE THEORY

RECAPITULATION OF THE THEORY

Based on consideration of the literature on gender-related expectations parents hold for their children and a theoretical orientation which suggests the impact of these expectations on parental control of the child's behavior, two primary hypotheses were developed for the study. Behavior was defined as gender-consistent or gender-inconsistent, depending upon the positive or negative quality of parental expectations and upon actual differences in the actions of boys and girls found in normative literature on the subject. The hypotheses predicted that gender-consistent behavior would be a more frequent target for abuse and would be more intense in form than gender-inconsistent behavior.

Results of the study do not support these hypotheses. In only two of the nine instances were parents more likely to abuse children for whom the behavior was gender-consistent. For only one of the four categories examined were parents more likely to abuse children exhibiting more extreme forms of the activity when it was gender-consistent. These findings raise serious questions concerning the utility of the theory and suggest that it is in need of revision.

POSSIBLE CONCLUSIONS

The research design used for the study did not allow for a direct test of the assumptions upon which hypotheses were based, so that conclusions concerning theory must be considered tentative pending further investigation. Three possible conclusions can be drawn with regard to the utility of these assumptions.

First, it may be argued that the theoretical orientation is valid but has been inadequately tested in this study. It is possible that the wrong population was chosen. Gender-related parental expectations may lead parents to punish children more often for gender-consistent behavior only in a normal population, not in an abusive one. We have argued that acceptable and unacceptable disciplinary practices lie on a continuum and that confusion exists concerning the point at which appropriate physical discipline becomes abusive. It was assumed that many of the events studied in this research are similar to those occurring in non-abusive families. However, it is possible that there is a qualitative difference between abuse and other types of physical control and that the interactive dynamics outlined in this paper do not occur in the former type of situation, although they do occur in the latter.

Without continued study using a control group consisting of non-abusive parents, this issue cannot be fully addressed. However, findings of the study pointing out that most abusive incidents involve beating the child (with the hand or an instrument) and produce minor subsequent injury to the child do suggest that, at least in terms of the actions of the parent in the situation, there is a strong resemblance between these incidents and spankings ad ministered in an acceptable way.

Perhaps it was inappropriate measurement of variables that produced misleading results. If complete and careful measures of behaviors could be obtained, it is possible that results would support the hypotheses outlined. The small amount of information available concerning each incident and the lack of validated measures are factors in the study providing support for this argument. Again, its utility could be tested only after more detailed examination of the dynamics of abuse in another research project. However, the number of negative findings for a variety of behavior categories does make this conclusion a questionable one.

The second possibility is that the theoretical orientation used in this study is completely inapplicable to the situation under consideration. Arguments here may involve several claims: the gender of the child may not be of any importance in abuse events; gender-related parental expectations may not play a role in such events; or gender-consistency or inconsistency of behavior may not be relevant for understanding of such situations.

These claims would have strong support if none of the results of the study were in accord with predictions outlined in the hypotheses. However, this does not prove to be the case. The very fact that parents tend to abuse boys more often than girls when children are young and to abuse more adolescent daughters suggests that gender-related factors are salient here. Moreover, of the nine behavior groups chosen for their significance in terms of gender-related parental expectations, differential abuse of male and female children did occur in four instances.

These findings suggest a third possible conclusion. That is, the theoretical orientation has some relevance for understanding the dynamics of abuse, although it is in need of extensive revision and greater specification. Recommended revisions of the theory based on findings of this research are outlined below.

NEW THEORETICAL VIEWPOINT

Findings of this research do not suggest a single explanation for the role of the gender of the child in abusive events. Results do indicate three major recommendations for future study of the part played by gender-related issues in such events.

BEHAVIOR-SPECIFIC THEORY

Results suggest that the relationship between the child's gender and behavior precipitating abuse is a complex one. There were gender differences in some of the behaviors examined but not in others. When such differences were found, they tended to be large. Girls were twice as likely to behave aggressively and to be in conflict with parents over performance of household taks, while boys were more than three times as likely to exhibit overactive behavior. However, no gender differences were found in five other behavior areas, including defiance, which was the most likely percursor of abuse in this study.

Three different types of activity appear to be present in abuse events, depending upon the age and gender of the child involved. (See Figure 5.) Defiance is a potent precursor of abuse for all children. Refusal to do something or stop doing it when told to do so is not attached to failure to perform any other particular type of task. It is possible that the refusal itself irritates parents and provides a justification in their eyes for subsequent severe discipline. The child's bid for independence and power in the family and the parent's fear of loss of control over the child may be factors contributing to maltreatment in such situations.

FIGURE 5
BEHAVIOR VARYING WITH AGE AND GENDER OF THE CHILD

GROUP I: GENERALLY UNACCEPTABLE BEHAVIOR
            Defiant Behavior

GROUP II: BEHAVIOR VARYING WITH AGE OF THE CHILD
            Subgroup I: Infants Displaying Emotional Upset
            Subgroup II: Older Children Displaying Aggression,
                         Achievement-Related Behaviors, Sociable
                         Behaviors

GROUP III: BEHAVIOR VARYING WITH GENDER OF THE CHILD
            Subgroup I: Adolescent Girls Acting Aggressively
            Subgroup II: Adolescent Girls in Conflict With Fathers
                          Over Sex-Related Behavior or Performance
                          of Household Tasks
            Subgroup III: Boys Engaging in Overactive and Physically
                          Aggressive Behaviors

Other behaviors appear more frequently for children of certain ages. For those younger than six, crying and other forms of emotional upset were precipitants of abuse in one out of every four events examined. Conflicts surrounding academic performance, aggressiveness and the ability to get along with others were of increasing salience as children matured. Key dynamics in these situations may involve conflicts between changing needs of maturing children and emerging expectations, hopes and fears of parents concerning the way their children will "turn out" as adults.

The third group of behaviors has special relevance for understanding the impact of the child's gender in abusive interaction. This category includes a variety of interactive patterns that may be explored. One of these concerns adolescent girls who are in conflict with their parents when they behave aggressively. A second subgroup includes adolescent daughters in conflict with their fathers over sex-related issues or housework. Other patterns describe boys who are overactive, behavior which seems to present more difficulties for mothers than fathers, and young boys who tend to be abused more than young girls, but for whom we have not found any specific types of behavior they are prone to exhibit.

It is likely that causes of abusive responses vary, depending upon the particular type of behavior considered. For example, when sex-related behaviors are at issue, fathers may be deeply concerned about detecting potential promiscuity in their daughters. Arousal of their own sexual feelings for their daughters may also provide a motivating force in this type of situation. On the other hand, when children behave aggressively, very different dynamics emerge. The "lippiness" of teenage girls may be intensely irritating to parents and difficult for them to ignore. Fear that this behavior will escalate into physical aggression probably also prompts severe disciplinary reactions.

Findings suggest that future study of the dynamics of abuse may be most fruitfully pursued through separate exploration of each of the nine categories (as well as others not considered in this study). Three behavioral areas may prove especially interesting in terms of understanding abuse and its causes. Defiant behavior is a common precipitant of abuse for children of all ages. Aggressive behavior requires further study because it, too, is a frequent precursor of abuse and because interactive components may differ for male and female children. Sex-related behaviors should be more fully examined in order to establish their association with sexual abuse and to shed light on parent-child confict patterns that emerge in families with adolescent daughters.

INTERVENING VARIABLE ANALYSIS

Figure 1 (page 16) depicts our initial attempt to define factors contributing to differential abuse of boys and girls. In that figure, general gender-related parental expectations were described as directly determining responses to behavior of sons and daughters. If parents expected different actions from boys and girls, it was argued, they would punish certain behaviors in line with these expectations.

Examination of results of this study suggests the presence of what Morris Rosenberg calls conditional relationships, situations where "the original relationship is more pronounced in one subgroup than in the other, when the total sample is divided by the test factor" (quoting Kendall and Lazarsfeld, 1968, p. 106). Under such conditions, intervening variables help clarify the relationship between independent and dependent variables by pointing out conditions in which their association is strengthened or weakened (Rosenberg, 1968).

In this study, one potential set of intervening factors are those discussed by Gelles in his study of violence in the family. He notes (1972) that parents develop specific rules for using violence on their children, rules which both parents and offspring are aware of and which parents attempt to enforce with some consistency. Gelles' finding leads us to question whether parents also develop a number of rules, some applicable only to boys or girls, others used with older or younger children. This disciplinary code may not be directly developed from parental gender-related expectations, although they probably play a role in its establishment. It is also possible that some of these expectations are not enforced through the use of physical disciplinary measures, while others become the basis for rules for using violence against children in the home.

A second group of factors intervening between specification of gender-related expectations and their application in abuse situations concern the characteristics of the particular child playing a role in the event. It is likely that parents develop — and adapt — their disciplinary code based on their perceptions of some particular areas in which a child requires correction. One boy in the family, perceived as extremely aggressive, may be spanked when displaying this activity, while another son, seen as too passive and quiet, may not be punished for engaging in the same behavior. Rules for using violence when children behave aggressively may exist in the family, although they may be differentially enforced, depending upon parental beliefs concerning needs of particular children.

These are not, of course, the only determinants of abusive parental behavior. A variety of other sources of stress within the family and the environment also escalate the likelihood of its occurrence. However, it is important to consider the role of these variables, since they suggest particular areas in which parents are frequently in conflict with their offspring, problems that may be long-standing and especially likely to precipitate abuse. Figure 6 depicts the impact of these factors in determining the nature of the interaction that occurs.

In some of the literature, abuse is described as sudden eruption into violent behavior in response to stresses that have little to do with the specific situation or child involved. In other writing, it is described as a fairly predictable, repetitive process that develops out of interaction between parents and children, behavior that can be understood through analysis of the characteristics of the participants. It is possible that abuse events of both types exist. Exploration of the role of parental expectations, disciplinary rules and characteristics of abused children will help clarify the circumstances under which these particular factors explain the development and continuation of abusive behavior in families.

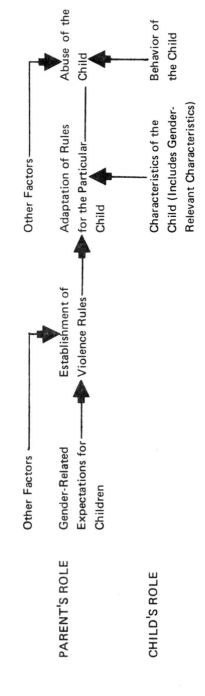

FIGURE 6

PROCESSES INVOLVED IN CHILD ABUSE CONTRIBUTING TO GENDER DIFFERENCES
IN BEHAVIOR OF CHILDREN IN ABUSIVE SITUATIONS

PARENT'S ROLE

Other Factors

Gender-Related
Expectations for
Children

Establishment of
Violence Rules

Other Factors

Adaptation of Rules
for the Particular
Child

Abuse of the
Child

CHILD'S ROLE

Characteristics of the
Child (Includes Gender-
Relevant Characteristics)

Behavior of
the Child

102

CONTROL VARIABLES

One major conclusion of this study is that abuse cannot be studied as a general, undifferentiated category of activity. Its nature and circumstances under which it occurs are extremely varied, as are its causes and consequences. Results suggest that age and gender of the child are two criteria that may be used to create sub-categories of abusive events for study. Age is especially important, since a number of abuse circumstances change, depending upon whether one is exploring incidents involving infants or adolescents. The behavior of the child and the nature and seriousness of the injury differ for these two groups. Characteristics of abuse also change if only boys or girls are included in the sample.

Gender of the parent is also a control variable of importance. Other factors of potential significance, which were not included in this report, concern the racial and cultural background of the family and the age of the abusive parent. Development of an adequate typology of maltreatment will depend upon development of data describing the impact of these and additional background factors on the structure and processes involved in parent-child interaction during these incidents.

FUTURE RESEARCH

Further exploration of the role of the child and the child's gender in abuse situations requires application of a more rigorous research design than the one used in this study. Since so many of the difficult questions concerning abuse deal with why and how it occurs, it is necessary that control groups of non-abusive parents be included for comparison purposes. Parents in such groups should be chosen from socio-economic backgrounds similar to those of publically identified abusive families, who tend to come from the less skilled, poorer segments of society.

Samples chosen for study should be large and representative since, as we have pointed out, abuse events tend to be highly variable in a number of their key characteristics. One cannot, for example, study a small number of cases of infant abuse and assume that findings are generally applicable to all mistreated children. Acquisition of adequate information also necessitates access to detailed data through use of carefully constructed case records or direct interviews with abusive family members.

SUMMARY

In this section, we have outlined some directives for future study of the role of the child's gender and behavior in abuse incidents. These recommendations are based on results of testing hypotheses in the study. They provide suggestions concerning the meaning of findings inconsistent with these hypotheses.

Three major recommendations are offered. First, consideration of specific types of children's behaviors that serve as precipitating factors in abuse situations will provide information about interactive patterns that frequently result in abuse. Second, assessment of family disciplinary rules, application of these rules to specific children in the family, and other characteristics of these children may prove useful intervening variables that help describe abusive processes. Third, inclusion of significant secondary independent variables, such as age of the child and gender of the parent, are necessary for adequate evaluation of the variety of types of abusive patterns that occur.

CHAPTER VII

CONCLUSION

We began and conclude this study by suggesting that a systems perspective is required for assessment of abusive events. Abuse is an interactive process in which the child and the parent play key roles. Little is, as yet, known about this process. To more fully explore it, research examining the behavior and characteristics of both the abused child and the abusive parent is required.

We have found that parents respond to very different types of behaviors exhibited by their children, depending upon such basic factors as the age and gender of these offspring. We have also reported that, in some cases, mothers and fathers abuse children who engage in different types of precipitating behaviors, although male and female parents frequently use severe disciplinary measures in response to very similar types of behavioral stimuli. The study was also designed to explore socio-economic differences in parent-child interaction. However, we were unable to adequately carry out this task due to the small number of middle and upper class families in the sample. Within the limited range of status levels considered, no social class differences were found.

These findings have relevance for social work practice in at least two respects. We are suggesting that social workers adopt the view that consideration of the characteristics of the child is of some importance in understanding abuse. This is not to be confused with blaming the child or with claiming that abuse can be understood only through study of the child. Instead, the child is presented here as playing only one of the primary roles in such incidents. Examination of this role will suggest points of intervention with both the parent and child in order to prevent further abuse.

The study is also of use to social work practitioners because it points out some parent-child interactive patterns that frequently occur in abuse situations and suggests differences in these patterns for boys and girls and for younger and older children. Interventive efforts are required to help parents cope with angry and defiant behavior exhibited by their children. Children also need assistance in recognizing this behavior may provoke unjustified extreme reactions from their parents. The study also points out that workers are frequently called upon to intervene in situations where problems of poverty must be dealt with along with difficulties in child-rearing.

We end this study with the recognition that there is much to learn about abusive events, their characteristics and variations, the nature of the actors in such events and the parts they play. Some suggestions have been offered for future research that we hope will shed new light on this complex, always painful, and sometimes tragic, sitiuation.

APPENDIX A

DATA COLLECTION INSTRUMENT

PART I. CASE IDENTIFICATION

1. Child's Name (Last, First, Middle)_____

2. Date Received_____ 3. County_____

4. Received from: 1 Reporter directly 2 Law Enforcement

5. First Reporter (to Law Enforcement or Agency)_____

   _____

   Street Address: _____

   Organization_____ City or Town_____

6. Reporter's Occupation or Relationship to Child:

   01 Physician 02 Nurse 03 Social Worker

   04 School Administrator, Counselor, Teacher, Soc. Wkr, Nurse

   05 Hosp. Administrator 06 Dentist 07 Law Enf. Officer

   08 Parent 09 Relative 10 Friend/Neighbor

   11 Other (Specify)_____

7. Child's Birth Date 8. Child's Sex: (1) Male (2) Female

9. Child's Race: (1) White (2) Black (3) Amer-Indian

   (4) Latin-American (5) Asian-American

   (6) Other (Specify)_____ (9) Unknown

10. Legal Mother's Name (Last, First, Middle)_____

    Street Address (Circle if child lives here)_____

    Birth Date_____ City or Town_____

    Maiden Name(Last)_____

    Previous Married Name (Last)_____

11. Legal Father's Name (Last, First, Middle)_____

    Street Address (Circle if child lives here)_____

    Birth Date_____ City or Town_____

12. Caretaker(s) (other than legal parents) Mother or Father Substitute in Household Where Child Lives_____

12. (Continued)

Street Address (Circle if Child Lives here_____

Age(s): ____(Male)____(Female)   City or Town_____

13. Caretaker(s) Relationship to Child:

Male Female

Male	Female	
1	1	Step parent
2	2	Foster parent
3	3	Relative
4	4	Other (specify)_____
8	8	Not applicable

14. Alleged Abuser(s) Name(s); if multiple alleged abusers, see instruction on back of form_____

Street Address_____

City or Town_____

Age(s) and Sex (as many as apply):   1st____age, ____sex

2nd____age, ____sex   3rd____age,____sex   4th____age, ____sex

15. Alleged Abuser(s) Relationship to Child:

1st	2nd		3rd	4th
1	1	Natural parent	1	1
2	2	Adopted parent	2	2
3	3	Step parent	3	3
4	4	Foster parent	4	4
5	5	Sibling	5	5
6	6	Other relative	6	6
7	7	Other (specify)	7	7
	8	Not applicable	8	8
9	9	Unknown	9	9

16. Worker's Immediate Plan:

1. Emergency (Investigate within ____hours)
2. Urgent (Follow-up within 24 hours)
3. Action needed (Follow within ____days)
4. No plan
   give reason:_____

17. CASE STATUS after follow-up

1	*No* injury or abuse	2	Injury but *no* abuse
3.	Abuse still uncertain	4	Abuse appears certain
5	Abuse legally established		

17. (Continued)

If Case Status 1 or 2, Stop Here

If Case Status 3, 4 or 5, Complete Entire Form

---

18. Case Type (Circle all that apply)

01 One child reported

02 More than one reported

04 More than one alleged abuser

08 Fatality

Worker's notation of objection to contact.

PART II. CHILD'S FAMILY BACKGROUND

19. Father or Substitute's Occupation/Education (Use Codes From Item

29 Below: Occupation_____   Education_____

20. Mother or Substitute's Occupation/Education (Use Codes From Item

29 Below: Occupation_____   Education_____

PART III. CHILD'S HOUSEHOLD At Time of Alleged Abuse

21. No. of Persons_____   22. No. of Rooms_____

23. No. of Adults

_____Legal Parents   _____Grandparents

_____Aunts, Uncles   _____Other related

_____Unknown if related   _____Not related

24. Other Children Residing in Household

No. Other Children   No. Previous Abused

_____ Natural Siblings   _____

_____ Siblings by Adoption   _____

_____ Half Siblings   _____

_____ Other Related   _____

_____ Foster Children   _____

_____ Other non-related   _____

No. older than child_____   Age of Oldest Child (if any older)___

No. younger than child_____   Age of Youngest (if any younger)____

109

PART IV. ALLEGED ABUSER'S BACKGROUND *For additional alleged
Abusers, use space at Bottom of Page

25. Abuse History:

a. Previous alleged abuse to child: (1) Same Child
   (2) Other child(ren)   (3) Same and other child(ren)
   (9) Unknown

b. Abuse to adults: (1) Yes or alleged   (2) No   (9) Unknown

c. Abused as a child: (1) Yes or alleged   (2) No   (9) Unknown

26. Birth Date_____

27. Race: (1) White   (2) Black   (3) Amer-Indian
     (4) Latin-American   (5) Asian-American
     (6) Other-specify_____   (9) Unknown

28. Occupation_____

29. Education (circle one code):   (0) None   (1) 8 years or less
     (2) 9-11 years   (3) H.S. grad   (4) Some College   (5) College grad
     (6) Vocational School in lieu of H.S.   (7) Other-specify)_____
     (9) Unknown

PART V. ALLEGED ABUSE (Circle ALL codes that apply)

30. Extent of injuries:

01 Bruises, welts	02 Sprains, dislocations
04 Bone fracture (not skull)	08 Internal injuries
16 Skull fracture	32 Brain damage

01 Psychological, emotion   02 Suffocation   04 Burns, scalding
08 Abrasions, lacerations   16 Cuts, punctures   32 Dismemberment
01 Freezing, exposure   02 Malnutrition
04 Sexual abuse (specify)_____
08 Other (specify)_____
00 None apparent

31. Evidence of previous abuse: (1) Yes   (2) Not apparent
     (9) Unknown

32. Judgment of Incident: 01 Beating with hands, slapping
     02 Beating with instruments   04 Kicking
     08 Throwing, pushing, droppins   16 Beating, hairpulling
     32 Tying up, locking in
     01 Strangling, suffocating   02 Drowning   04 Burning, scalding

36. Welfare Services to family (circle all codes that apply)

001 Casework Services   002 Guidance Clinic or Counseling Clinic
004 Financial Assistance and planning   008 Public Medical Care
016 Maternity Care   032 Day Care Services   064 Homemaker Services
028 Other (specify)
000 Services never given   999 Unknown

37. Placement of Child (circle one code only)
(1) Removed from home but later returned
(2) Moved to relative's home   (3) Moved to foster home
(4) Institutionalized (specify)
(5) Indeterminate, child still hospitalized   (6) Child died
(7) Child not placed, remained at home   (9) Unknown
(8) Other (specify)

38. Placement of other children
1 All removed from home   2 Some removed from home
3 No children removed   8 Not applicable, no other children
9 Unknown

39. Juvenile Court Action (circle one code only)
1 No court referral   2 Petition dismissed
3 Child at home under supervision   4 Custody transferred
5 Guardianship transferred   6 Petition: no action taken
7 Other (specify)

40. Criminal Court Action (circle one code only)
1 No referral to DA   2 Referral to DA, no court referral
3 Complaint dismissed   4 Legal Sentence, date
5 Referral to court: no action taken
6 Other (specify)

41. Please add a paragraph on:
1) What precipitated the alleged abuse
2) The alleged abuse incident

ment in systems including the family but part is also due to the negative complications of the attitude that society takes responsibility for its youth versus the conception that adults need to take responsibility for their society.

There are numerous good programs for youth that are effective in promoting some healthy personal growth, stability, reintegration into school, family, community groups, etc. They often utilize a consistent, well developed theoretical model which is implemented by a highly trained, skillful staff. However, they seldom have the flexibility to be effective with a varied clientele. It would be gratifying to report that the only two long-term residential facilities for youth in prostitution have been successful by virtue of their specialization in this area but that is not possible at present.

One must separate the complexities of providing psychotherapy with adolescents in general from the difficulties germane to a clientele of adolescents in prostitution and then further delineate specific programmatic concerns. A thorough analysis is beyond the scope of this text but the allusions are necessary for illumination. The first facility for juveniles in prostitution was based in Minneapolis and closed after two years, marred by administrative turnover, in-house fighting among staff and numerous other personnel problems. It has recently resumed operation after a period of abandonment due to community interest. The second program operating in Denver since February 1982 has suffered similar personnel problems and program revamping. It may yet succeed but much more time is necessary to glean conclusive evidence of worth.

Many of the program problems are a natural consequence of inherent difficulties that plague small, community-based efforts. Quality care depends almost exclusively on personnel. The organization often lacks professionalism since it is not large enough to train properly, recruit the needed initial expertise and absorb the impact of negative influences that can be minimized in more substantial programs. There is also the constant political environment promoted by the need for funding and

APPENDIX B

TABLES

TABLE 1

AGE OF ABUSIVE PARENT

AGE	FREQUENCY	PERCENT
19 or less	11	1.4%
20-24-1/2	110	14.0%
25-29-1/2	167	21.3%
30-34-1/2	178	22.7%
35-39-1/2	145	18.5%
40-44-1/2	83	10.6%
45-49-1/2	51	6.5%
50 or older	39	5.0%
TOTAL	784	100.0%

Missing Cases = 46

TABLE 2

OCCUPATIONS OF MALE AND FEMALE ABUSIVE PARENTS

	GENDER	
OCCUPATIONS	MALE	FEMALE
Major Professional	2.0% (9)	0.0% (0)
Minor Professional	9.1% (42)	2.5% (8)
Clerical	8.2% (38)	10.0% (32)
Skilled Laborer	16.1% (74)	1.9% (6)
Semi-Skilled Laborer	17.6% (81)	6.9% (22)
Unskilled Laborer	31.7% (146)	9.7% (31)
Homemaker	.4% (2)	55.9% (179)
Unemployed	15.0% (69)	13.1% (42)
TOTAL	100.0% (461)	100.0% (320)

Chi square = 365.046, d.f. = 7, p = .0000
N = 781 (49 Cases Missing)

116

TABLE 3

METHODS MALE AND FEMALE ABUSERS USED
TO INFLICT INJURY ON THE CHILD

	GENDER	
ABUSE METHODS USED	MALE	FEMALE
Beat with Hands, Slapped	43.0%	26.0%
	(206)	(84)
Beat with Instrument	38.0%	55.1%
	(182)	(178)
Kicked	5.2%	1.9%
	(25)	(6)
Threw, Pushed, Dropped	9.4%	7.4%
	(45)	(24)
Bit, Pulled Hair, Scratched	1.3%	2.8%
	(6)	(9)
Tied Up, Locked In	0.0%	2.5%
	(0)	(8)
Strangled, Suffocated, Burned	3.1%	4.0%
	(15)	(13)
Shot, Stabbed, Slashed	0.0%	.3%
	(0)	(1)
TOTAL	100.0%	100.0%
	(479)	(323)

Chi square = 50.723, d.f. = 7, p = .0000
N = 802 (28 Cases Missing)

TABLE 4

ABUSE METHODS USED BY AGE OF CHILD

	AGE OF CHILD		
ABUSE METHODS USED	INFANCY	LATENCY	ADOLESCENCE
Beat with Hands, Slapped	42.8%	26.8%	38.8%
	(95)	(73)	(108)
Beat with Instrument	36.0%	57.0%	41.7%
	(80)	(155)	(116)
Kicked	.9%	4.0%	5.8%
	(2)	(11)	(16)
Threw, Pushed, Dropped	10.8%	6.6%	8.6%
	(24)	(18)	(24)
Bit, Pulled Hair, Scratched	2.3%	1.1%	2.2%
	(5)	(3)	(6)
Tied Up, Locked In	2.7%	.7%	0.0%
	(6)	(2)	(0)
Strangled, Suffocated, Burned	4.5%	3.3%	2.9%
	(10)	(9)	(8)
Shot, Stabbed, Slashed	0.0%	.4%	0.0%
	(0)	(1)	(0)
TOTAL	100.0%	100.0%	100.0%
	(222)	(272)	(278)

Chi square = 46.416, d.f. = 14, p = .0000
N = 772 (58 Cases Missing)

TABLE 5

TYPE OF INJURY SUSTAINED BY AGE OF CHILD

TYPE OF INJURY	AGE OF CHILD		
	INFANCY	LATENCY	ADOLESCENCE
Bruises, Welts	76.7%	78.0%	81.5%
	(161)	(202)	(211)
Sprains, Dislocations	.5%	0.0%	2.3%
	(1)	(0)	(6)
Abrasions, Lacerations	6.7%	12.4%	8.5%
	(14)	(32)	(22)
Cuts, Punctures	5.7%	5.0%	6.6%
	(12)	(13)	(17)
Bone Fractures	2.9%	1.2%	.4%
	(6)	(3)	(1)
Skull Fractures	3.3%	.4%	0.0%
	(7)	(1)	(0)
Suffocation, Burns, Scalding	3.8%	3.1%	.4%
	(8)	(8)	(1)
Sexual Abuse	.5%	0.0%	.4%
	(1)	(0)	(1)
TOTAL	100.0%	100.0%	100.0%
	(210)	(259)	(259)

Chi square = 40.002, d.f. = 14, p = .0003
N = 728 (102 Cases Missing)

TABLE 6
CORRELATIONS AMONG DEPENDENT VARIABLES

	Aggression	Active Behavior	Defiance	Emotional Upset	Achievement	Sociable	Appearance	Housework	Sex-Related
Aggression	r=1.000 S=.001	r=-.059 S=.089	r=-.049 S=.169	r=-.134 S=.001	r=.020 S=.558	r=.113 S=.001	r=.027 S=.432	r=.042 S=.229	r=.042 S=.225
Active Behavior		r=1.000 S=.001	r=.067 S=.053	r=-.065 S=.061	r=-.055 S=.112	r=-.027 S=.441	r=-.029 S=.399	r=-.016 S=.643	r=-.047 S=.173
Defiance			r=1.000 S=.001	r=-.031 S=.379	r=-.090 S=.009	r=.011 S=.762	r=.113 S=.001	r=.171 S=.001	r=-.066 S=.056
Emotional Upset				r=1.000 S=.001	r=-.059 S=.090	r=-.054 S=.121	r=-.041 S=.240	r=-.085 S=.015	r=-.045 S=.194
Achievement					r=1.000 S=.001	r=-.018 S=.602	r=-.035 S=.318	r=-.053 S=.128	r=-.032 S=.357
Sociable						r=1.000 S=.001	r=-.033 S=.344	r=.073 S=.035	r=-.028 S=.423
Appearance							r=1.000 S=.001	r=-.038 S=.272	r=.014 S=.697
Housework								r=1.000 S=.001	r=-.040 S=.254
Sex-Related									r=1.000 S=.001

(d.f. = 828 For Each Correlation)

TABLE 7
AGE OF CHILD AND BEHAVIORS PRECIPITATING ABUSE

AGE OF CHILD
(% of Cases Behavior Present)

Behavior Category	Infancy	Latency	Adolescence	Significance Level
Aggression	8.2%	13.0%	35.0%	Chi Square= 70.232
	(19)	(37)	(99)	d.f =2, p=.0000
Active Behaviors	6.4%	5.3%	2.1%	N.S
	(15)	(15)	(6)	
Defiance	19.7%	21.5%	18.7%	N.S
	(46)	(61)	(53)	
Expression of	25.8%	1.1%	1.1%	Chi square
Emotional Upset	(60)	(3)	(3)	133.025, d f =2.
				p = .0000
Achievement-Related	.4%	7.7%	9.2%	Chi square= 19.061
Behaviors	(1)	(22)	(26)	d.f.=2, p=.0000
Sociable Behaviors	1.7%	5.3%	8.8%	Chi square=12.495
	(4)	(15)	(25)	d.f.=2, p=.0019
Behaviors Reflecting on	.4%	1.8%	3.2%	N S
Personal Appearance	(1)	(5)	(9)	
Performance of	2.1%	6.7%	12.4%	Chi square=19.847
Household Tasks	(5)	(19)	(35)	d.f.=2, p=.0000
Sex-Related	1.3%	1.1%	11.0%	Chi square=39.782
Behaviors	(3)	(3)	(31)	d.f.=2, p=.0000
	N=233	N=284	N=283	N=800

TABLE 8
PARTIAL CORRELATIONS: GENDER AND BEHAVIOR OF CHILD, CONTROLLING FOR SECONDARY INDEPENDENT VARIABLES

Behavior Category	CORRELATIONS Gender of Child	PARTIAL CORRELATIONS Age of Child	Gender of Parent	Family Social Class
Aggression	-.157	-.085	-.157	-.157
	S=.001	S=.017	S=.001	S=.001
Active Behaviors	.121	.102	.122	.119
	S=.001	S=.004	S=.001	S=.003
Defiance	.001	.004	.001	-.001
	S=.969	S=.911	S=.970	S=.984
Emotional Upset	.026	-.096	.026	.024
	S=.462	S=.006	S=.461	S=.553
Achievement	.010	.048	.010	.009
	S=.766	S=.180	S=.765	S=.827
Sociable Behaviors	-.050	-.016	-.050	-.045
	S=.150	S=.650	S=.151	S=.263
Personal Appearance	.023	.044	.023	.021
	S=.516	S=.220	S=.513	S=.593
Household Tasks	-.088	-.050	-.088	-.088
	S=.011	S=.155	S=.011	S=.028
Sex-Related Behaviors	-.187	-.140	-.187	-.186
	S=.001	S=.001	S=.001	S=.001
d.f. =	826	796	825	629

122

BIBLIOGRAPHY

Aleksandrowicz, M. & D. The Molding of Personality. *Child Psychiatry and Human Development*, 1975, 5, 231-241.

Alvy, K. Preventing Child Abuse. *American Psychologist*, 1975, 921-928

American Humane Association. *National Analysis of Official Child Neglect and Abuse Reporting*. Denver: Center for Social Research and Development, 1978.

Bakan, D. *Slaughter of the Innocents: A Study of the Battered-Child Syndrome*. San Francisco: Jossey Bass, 1971.

Bandura, A. & Walters, R. Aggression. in Stevenson, H., Kagan, J. & Spiker, C., Eds. *Child Psychology: Part I*. Chicago: University of Chicago Press, 1963, 364-415.

Barry, H., Bacon, M. & Child, I. A Cross-Cultural Survey of Some Sex Differences in Socialization. in Lee, P. & Stewart, R.S., Eds. *Sex Differences: Cultural and Developmental Dimensions*. NY: Urizen Books, 1976, 218-228.

Baruch, G. Sex-Role Stereotyping, the Motive to Avoid Success and Parental Identification. *Sex Roles*, 1975, 1, 303-309.

Baumtrog, C. Early Child Abuse and Adolescence. *Center for Youth Development and Research: Quarterly Focus*, 1975, 207-213.

Becker, W. Consequences of Different Kinds of Parental Discipline. in Hoffman, M. & L., Eds. *Review of Child Development Research: Vol. 1.* NY: Russell Sage, 1964, 169-208.

Beckwith, L. Relationships Between Infants' Social Behavior and Their Mother's Behavior. *Child Development*, 1972, 43, 397-411.

Bell, G. Parents Who Abuse Their Children. *Canadian Psychiatric Association Journal*, 1973, 18, 223-228.

Bell, R. Reinterpretation of the Direction of Effects in Studies of Socialization. *Psychological Review*, 1968, 75, 81-95.

Bennie, E. H. & Sclare, A. B. The Battered Child Syndrome. *American Journal of Psychiatry*, 1969, 125, 147-151.

Berkowitz, L. *Aggression: A Social Psychological Analysis.* NY: McGraw Hill, 1962.

Berkowitz, L. Control of Aggression. in Caldwell, B. & Ricciuti, N., Eds. *Review of Child Development Research: Vol. 3.* Chicago: University of Chicago Press, 1973, 95-140.

Bishop, F. I. Children at Risk. *Medical Journal of Australia*, 1971, 623-628.

Block, J. Conceptions of Sex Role: Some Cross-Cultural and Longitudinal Perspectives. *American Psychologist*, 1973, 512-526.

Block, J. *Another Look at Sex Differentiation in the Socialization Behaviors of Mothers and Fathers.* Paper presented at conference on New Directions for Research on Women, Madison, Wisconsin, May, 1975.

Block, J. Issues, Problems and Pitfalls in Assessing Sex Differences

A Critical Review of The Psychology of Sex Differences. *Merrill-Palmer Quarterly*, 1976, 22, 283-308.

Boisvert, M. The Battered-Child Syndrome. *Social Casework*, 1972, 475-480.

Bowerman, C. & Kinch, J. Changes in Family and Peer Orientation of Children Between the Fourth and Tenth Grades. *Social Forces*, 1959, 37, 206-211.

Brocker, C. *Resolution of Child Abuse: A Process Analysis*. Unpublished doctoral dissertation, Univ. of Wisconsin, Madison, 1977.

Bronfenbrenner, U. Toward a Theoretical Model for the Analysis of Parent-Child Relationships in a Social Context. in Glidewell, J., Ed. *Parental Attitudes and Child Behavior*. Springfield, IL: Charles C. Thomas, 1961, 90-109.

Bryant, H. et al. Physical Abuse of Children — An Agency Study. *Child Welfare*, 1963, 42, 125-130.

Campbell, D. & Stanley, J. *Experimental and Quasi-Experimental Designs for Research*. Chicago: Rand McNally, 1973.

Clausen, J. & Williams, J. Sociological Correlates of Child Behavior. in Stevenson, H., Kagan, J. & Spiker, C., Eds. *Child Psychology: Part I*. Chicago: Univ. of Chicago Press, 1963, 62-107;

Conger, J. J. *Adolescence and Youth: Psychological Development in a Changing World*. NY: Harper & Ros, 1973.

Delsordo, J. Protective Casework for Abused Children. *Children*, 1963, 10, 213-218.

Deutsch, C. Social Class and Child Development. in Caldwell, B.

& Ricciuti, N., Eds. *Review of Child Development Research, Vol. 3.* Chicago: University of Chicago Press, 1973, 233-282

Division of Family Services. *Child Abuse in Wisconsin: 1974.* Madison, Wisconsin: no date.

Division of Family Services. *Child Abuse in Wisconsin: 1975.* Madison, Wisconsin, no date.

Elmer, E. *Child Abuse: Overview of the Problem and Avenues of Attack.* Paper presented at the Fifth Annual Mental Health Institute, July, 1966.

Elmer, E. et al. Studies of Child Abuse and Infant Accidents. in Segal, J., Ed. *Mental Health of the Child.* Maryland: National Institute of Mental Health, 1971, 343-370.

Erlanger, H. Social Class and Corporal Punishment in Childrearing: A Reassessment. *American Sociological Review*, 1974, 39, 68-85.

Eron, L., Huesmann, L. R., Lefkowitz, M. & Walder, L. How Learning Conditions in Early Childhood - Including Mass Media - Relate to Aggression in Late Adolescence. *American Journal of Orthopsychiatry*, 1974, 44, 412-423.

Feshback, S. Aggression. in Mussen, P., Ed. *Carmichael's Manual of Child Psychology: Vol. 2.* NY: Wiley, 1970, 159-245.

Flynn, W. Frontier Justice: A Contribution to the Theory of Child Battering. *American Journal of Psychiatry*, 1970, 127, 375-379.

Frankiel, R. *A Review of Research on Parent Influences on Child Personality.* NY: Family Service Association of America, 1959.

Freeman, D. The Battering Parent and His Child: A Study of Early Object Relations. *International Review of Psychoanalysis*, 1975, 2, 189-197.

Friedrich, W. & Boriskin, J. The Role of the Child in Abuse. *American Journal of Orthopsychiatry*, 1976, 46, 580-590.

Frodi, A., Macaulay, J. & Thome, P. Are Women Always Less Aggressive Than Men? A Review of the Experimental Literature. *Psychological Bulletin*, 1977.

Galdston, R. Observations on Children Who Have Been Physically Abused and Their Parents. *American Journal of Psychiatry*, 1965, 122, 440-443.

Galdston, R. Dysfunctions of Parenting: The Battered Child, The Neglected Child, The Exploited Child. in Howell, J., Ed. *Modern Perspectives in International Child Psychiatry*. Edinburgh: Oliver & Boyd, 1969, 571-588.

Galdston, R. Preventing the Abuse of Little Children. *American Journal of Orthopsychiatry*, 1975, 45, 372-381.

Gelles, R. *The Violent Home: A Study of Physical Aggression Between Husbands and Wives*. Beverly Hills, California: Sage Publications, 1972.

Gelles, R. *Violence Towards Children in the United States*. Paper presented at symposium on Violence at Home and at School, American Association for the Advancement of Science, Denver, February, 1977.

Gesell, A. & Ilg, F. Sex and Self. in Lee, P. & Stewart, R. S., Eds. *Sex Differences: Cultural and Developmental Dimensions*. NY: Urizen Books, 1976, 418-422.

Gil, D. *Violence Against Children: Physical Child Abuse in the*

United States. Cambridge, MA: Harvard Univ. Press, 1970.

Gil, D. A Sociocultural Perspective on Physical Child Abuse. *Child Welfare*. 1971, 50, 389-395.

Gil, D. Unraveling Child Abuse. *American Journal of Orthopsychiatry*, 1975, 45, 346-356.

Green, A. Psychodynamic Approach to the Study and Treatment of Child Abusing Parents. *American Academy of Child Psychiatry*, 1976, 414-429.

Green, A., Gaines, R. & Sandgrund, A. Child Abuse: Pathological Syndrome of Family Interaction. *American Journal of Psychiatry*, 1974, 131, 882-886.

Group for the Advancement of Psychiatry. *Psychopathological Disorders of Childhood: Theoretical Considerations and a Proposed Classification*. NY: Jason Aronson, 1966.

Hartup, W. Dependence and Independence. in Stevenson, H., Kagan, J. & Spiker, C., Eds. *Child Psychology: Part I.* Chicago: Univ. of Chicago Press, 1963, 333-363.

Hauser, R. & Featherman, D. *The Process of Stratification: Trends and Analysis*. NY: Academic Press, 1977.

Helfer, R. Etiology of Child Abuse. *Pediatrics*, 1973, 51, 777-779.

Herbst, P. G. The Measurement of Family Relationships. *Human Relations*, 1952, 5, 3-35.

Hoffman, M. Conscience, Personality and Socialization Techniques *Human Development*, 1970a, 13, 90-126.

Hoffman, M. Moral Development. in Mussen, P., Ed. *Carmichael's*

Manual of Child Psychology: Vol. 2. NY: Wiley, 1970b, 261-349.

Hurt, M. *Child Abuse and Neglect: A Report of the Status of the Research.* Washington, D.C.: Government Printing Office, 1975. (H.E.W. Publ. No. (OHD) 74-20).

Johnson, B. & Morse, H. Injured Children and Their Parents. *Children,* 1968, 15, 147-152.

Kadushin, A. & Berkowitz, L. *The Child's Contribution to Abuse* Grant Proposal submitted to NIMH: Funded, 1976.

Kagan, J. Acquisition and Significance of Sex Typing and Sex Role Identity in Hoffman, M. & L., Eds. *Review of Child Development Research: Vol. 1.* NY: Russell Sage, 1964, 137-167.

Kempe, H. & Helfer, R. *Helping the Battered Child and His Family.* Philadelphia: J.B. Lippincott, 1972.

Kerlinger, F. *Foundations of Behavioral Research.* NY: Holt, Rinehart & Winston, 1973.

Kohlberg, L. Moral Development and Identification. in Stevenson, H., H., Kagan, J. & Spiker, C., Eds. *Child Psychology: Part I.* Chicago: Univ. of Chicago Press, 1963, 277-332.

Kohlberg, L. Development of Moral Character and Moral Ideology. in Hoffman, M. & L., Eds. *Review of Child Development Research: Vol. 1.* NY: Russell Sage, 1964, 383-431.

Kohlberg, L. & Zigler, E. Physiological Development, Cognitive Development, and Socialization Antecedents of Children's Sex-Role Attitudes. in Lee, P. & Stewart, R. S., Eds. *Sex Differences: Cultural and Developmental Dimensions.* NY: Urizen Books, 1976, 435-443.

Kohn, M. & Rosman, B. A Social Competence Scale and Symptom Checklist for the Preschool Child. *Developmental Psychology*, 1972, 6, 430-444.

Korsch, B., Christian, J., Gozzi, E. & Carlson, P. Infant Care and Punishment: A Pilot Study. *American Journal of Public Health*, 1965, 55, 1880-1888.

Lamb, M. *The Two Factor Index of Social Position*. Unpublished paper, no date.

Lapouse, R. & Monk, M. An Epidemologic Study of Behavior Characteristics in Children. *American Journal of Public Health*, 1968, 58, 1134-1144.

Lauer, B., TenBroeck, E., & Grossman, M. Battered Child Syndrome: A Review of 130 Patients with Controls. *Pediatrics*, 1974, 54, 67-70.

Laury, G. The Battered Child Syndrome: Parental Motivation, Clinical Aspects. *Bulletin of the New York Academy of Medicine*, 1970, 676-685.

Lee, P. & Stewart, R. S. *Sex Differences: Cultural and Developmental Dimensions*. NY: Urizen Books, 1976.

Lefkowitz, M., Walder, L. & Eron, L. Punishment, Identification and Aggression. *Merrill-Palmer Quarterly*, 1963, 9, 159-174.

LeMasters, E. E. *Parents in Modern America: A Sociological Analysis*. Homewood, IL: Dorsey Press, 1970.

Lenoski, E. F., *Child Abuse*. Unpublished paper, no date.

Linton, R. The Study of Man. in Lee, P. & Stewart, R. S., Eds. *Sex Differences: Cultural and Developmental Dimensions*. NY: Urizen Books, 1976, 171-191.

Lord, E. & Weisfeld. The Abused Child. in Roberts, A., Ed. *Childhood Deprivation*. Springfield, IL: Charles Thomas, 1974, 76-79.

Maccoby, E. & Jacklin, C. *The Psychology of Sex Differences*. Stanford: Stanford Univ. Press, 1974.

Maccoby, E. & Masters, J. Attachment and Dependency. in Mussen, P., Ed. *Carmichael's Manual of Child Psychology: Vol. 2*. NY: Wiley, 1970, 73-157.

Martin, H. The Child and HIs Development. in Kempe, H. & Helfer, R., Eds. *Helping the Battered Child and His Family*. Philadelphia: J. B. Lippincott, 1972, 93-112.

Martin, H. & Beezley, P. Prevention and the Consequences of Child Abuse. *Journal of Operational Psychiatry*, 1974, 6, 68-77.

Matteson, D. *Adolescence Today: Sex Roles and the Search for Identity*. Homewood, IL: Dorsey Press, 1975.

Megargee, E. A Critical Review of Theories of Violence. in Mulvihill, D.J. & Tumin, M.M., Eds. *Crimes of Violence: Vol. 13*. Staff Report submitted to the National Commission on the Causes and Prevention of Violence, Dec., 1969, 1037-1115.

Newman, B. & P. *Development Through LIfe: A Psychosocial Approach*. Homewood, IL: Dorsey Press, 1975.

Nie, N., Hull, C. H., Jenkins, J., Steinbrenner, K. & Bent, D. *Statistical Package for the Social Sciences: Second Edition*. NY: McGraw-Hill, 1975.

Oghalai, K. *Ten Year Summary of Child Abuse Reporting in Wisconsin: 1967-1976*. Madison, WI: Dept. of Health and Social Services, no date.

Papajohn, J. & Spiegel, J. *Transactions in Families*. San Francisco: Jossey Bass, 1975.

Parke, R. Rules, Roles and Resistance to Deviation: Recent Advances in Punishment, Discipline and Self-Control. *Minnesota Symposium on Child Psychology*, 1974, 8, 111-143.

Parke, R. & Collmer, C. W. *Child Abuse: An Interdisciplinary Analysis*. Chicago: Univ. of Chicago Press, 1975.

Paulson, M. & Blake, P. The Physically Abused Child: A Focus on Prevention. *Child Welfare*, 1969, 48, 86-95.

Resnick, P. Child Murder by Parents: A Psychiatric Review of Filicide. *American Journal of Psychiatry*, 1969, 126, 325-334.

Robson, K. & Moss, H. Patterns and Determinants of Maternal Attachment. *Journal of Pediatrics*, 1970, 77, 976-985.

Rosenberg, F. & Simmons, R. Sex Differences in the Self-Concept in Adolescence. *Sex Roles*, 1975, 1, 147-159.

Rosenberg, M. *The Logic of Survey Analysis*. NY: Basic Books, 1968.

Rosenthal, M. The Study of Infant-Environment Interaction: Some Comments on Trends and Methodologies. *Journal of Child Psychology and Psychiatry*, 1973, 14, 301-317.

Roth, F. A Practice Regimen for Diagnosis and Treatment of Child Abuse. *Child Welfare*, 1975, 54, 268-273.

Schonell, F. & Watts, B. H. A First Survey of the Effects of a Subnormal Child on the Family Unit. *American Journal of Mental Deficiency*, 1956-1957, 61, 210-219.

Schultz, L. G. The Victim-Offender Relationship. *Crime and Delinquency*, 1968, 14, 135-141.

Seavy, C., Katz, P. & Zalk, S. R. Baby X: The Effect of Gender Labels on Adult Responses to Infants. *Sex Roles*, 1975, 1, 103-109.

Sellin, T. A Sociological Approach to the Study of Crime Causation. in Wolfgang, M., Savitz, L. & Johnston, N., Eds. *The Sociology of Crime and Delinquency*. NY: Wiley, 1962, 3-9.

Seltiz, C., Wrightsman, L. S. & Cook, S.W. *Research Methods in Social Relations: Third Edition*. NY: Holt, Rinehart & Winston, 1976.

Siegel, S. *Nonparametric Statistics for the Behavioral Sciences*. NY: McGraw Hill, 1956.

Silver, L., Dublin, C. & Lourie, R. Does Violence Breed Violence? Contributions from a Study of the Child Abuse Syndrome. *American Journal of Psychiatry*, 1969, 126, 152-155.

Skinner, A. & Castle, R. *78 Battered Children: A Retrospective Study*. London: National Society for the Prevention of Cruelty to Children, 1969.

Spinetta, J. & Rigler, D. The Child Abusing Parent: A Psychological Review. *Psychological Bulletin*, 1972, 77, 296-304.

Steele, B. F. & Pollock, C.B. A Psychiatric Study of Parents Who Abuse Infants and Small Children. in Helfer, R. & Kempe, R., Eds. *The Battered Child*. Chicago: Univ. of Chicago Press, 1968, 103-144.

Stone, L. J. & Church, J. *Childhood and Adolescence*. NY: Random House, 1968.

Straus, M. Some Social Antecedents of Physical Punishment: A Linkage Theory Interpretation. *Journal of Marriage and the Family*, 1971, 33, 658-663.

Strodtbeck, F. Family Interaction, Values and Achievement. in McClelland, D., Baldwin, A., Bronfenbrenner, U. & Strodtbeck, F., Eds. *Talent and Society*. Princeton, D. Van Nostrand, 1958, 135-194.

Sutherland, E. & Cressey, D. *Principles of Criminology: Seventh Edition*. Philadelphia: J. B. Lippincott, 1966.

Terman, L. & Miles, C. C. Sex and Personality: Studies in Masculinity and Feminity. in Lee, P. & Stewart, R.S., Eds. *Sex Differences: Cultural and Developmental Dimensions*. NY: Urizen Books, 1976, 383-394.

Terr, L. A Family Study of Child Abuse. *American Journal of Psychiatry*, 1970, 127, 665-671.

Tyler, L. Sex Differences in Personality Characteristics. in Lee, P. & Stewart, R. S., Eds. *Sex Differences: Cultural and Developmental Dimensions*. NY: Urizen Books, 1976, 395-410.

Walters, J. & Stinnett, N. Parent Child Relationships: A Decade Review of Research. *Journal of Marriage and the Family*, 1971, 33, 70-118.

Weinberg, G. Some Common Assumptions Underlying Traditional Child Psychotherapy: Fallacy and Reformulation. *Psychotherapy: Theory, Research and Practice*, 1972, 9, 149-152.

Williams, J. W. & Stith, M. *Middle Childhood: Behavior and Development*. NY: Macmillan, 1974.

Yarrow, M., Campbell, J. & Burton, R. *Child Rearing: An Inquiry Into Research and Methods*. SF: Jossey Bass, 1968.

Yarrow, M. & Waxler, C. Child Effects on Adult Behavior. *Developmental Psychology*, 1971, 5, 300-311.

Young, L. *Wednesday's Children: A Study of Child Neglect and Abuse*. NY: McGraw Hill, 1964.

Zalba, S. R. The Abused Child I: A Survey of the Problem. *Social Work*, 1966, 11, 3-16.

Zalba, S. The Abused Child II: A Typology for Classification and Treatment. *Social Work*, 1967, 12, 70-79.

Zeldow, P. & Greenberg, R. The Process of Sex Attribution. *Sex Roles*, 1975, 1, 111-120.

DATE			
DEC 1 1 1984			APR 0 6 1990
MAR 5 - 1985	FEB 1 9 1987		APR 1 0 1991
APR 0 3 1985	Mar 9/87.		NOV 2 1 1991
APR 0 9 1985	MAR 2 5 1987		APR 1 3 1994
APR 2 2 1985	MAR 2 6 1907		MAR 1 8 1995
DEC 0 2 1985	NOV 1 7 1987		MAR 0 6 1995
	DEC 8 1987		APR 1 3